VFR & IFR COMMUNICATIONS

Stuart E. Smith

STUDY GUIDE SERIES for EASA PART-FCL examinations

British Library Cataloguing in Publication Data.
A catalogue record for this book is pending from the British Library.

First published in the United Kingdom by Cranfield Aviation Training School Limited. 2002

Further volumes in this series are:
Aircraft General Knowledge: Airframes / Systems / Powerplant / Electrics / Emergency Equipment
Aviation Law & ATC Procedures
Flight Planning & Monitoring
General Navigation
Human Performance & Limitations
Instruments & Electronics
Mass & Balance
Meteorology
Operational Procedures
Performance
Principles of Flight
Radio Navigation

Series editor: Dr. Stuart E. Smith

CRANFIELD AVIATION TRAINING SCHOOL LTD. PART-FCL ATO N° 0136
CATS INNOVATION CENTRE, LUTON, Bedfordshire LU2 8DL U.K.

www.catsaviation.com

Communications

How to Study VFR Communications		iv
How to Study IFR Communications		iv
CHAPTER 1 Definitions and Abbreviations		1-1
1.1	Stations	1-1
1.2	Communication Methods	1-1
1.3	Miscellaneous Definitions	1-1
1.4	Air Traffic Control Abbreviations	1-4
CHAPTER 2 Communication Systems		2-1
2.1	General	2-1
2.1.1	Operation	2-1
2.2	Aeronautical Mobile Service	2-1
2.2.1	Definition	2-1
2.2.2	Radio Communication Discipline	2-1
2.2.3	Duration of Communication	2-2
CHAPTER 3 Q-Codes		3-1
3.1	Request for service	3-1
3.2	Common Q-Codes	3-1
3.2.1	Pressure Settings	3-1
3.2.2	Directions and bearings	3-1
3.2.3	Accuracy of Bearings and Positions	3-1
3.2.3.1	Bearings	3-2
3.2.3.2	Positions	3-2
CHAPTER 4 Categories of Messages		4-1
4.1	Priority of messages	4-1
4.1.1	Distress Messages	4-1
4.1.2	Urgency Messages	4-1
4.1.3	Direction Finding	4-1
4.1.4	Flight Safety Messages	4-1
4.1.5	Meteorological Messages	4-2
4.1.6	Flight Regularity Messages	4-2
CHAPTER 5 General Operating Procedures		5-1
5.1	Transmission of Letters	5-1
5.2	Transmission of Numbers	5-2
5.3	Transmission of Time	5-3
5.4	Transmitting Techniques	5-3
5.4.1	Stuck microphone	5-3
CHAPTER 6 Standard Phraseology		6-1
6.1	Standard Words and Phrases	6-1
6.2	Aerodrome Procedures	6-2
6.2.1	Departure Information and Engine Starting Procedures	6-2
6.2.2	Taxi Instructions	6-4
6.2.3	Take-Off Procedures	6-5
6.2.4	Aerodrome Traffic Circuit	6-9
6.2.5	Final Approach and Landing	6-12
6.2.6	Go Around	6-14
6.2.7	After Landing	6-15
6.2.8	Essential Aerodrome Information	6-15
6.3	VFR Departures	6-16
6.4	VFR Arrivals	6-17
6.5	Call Signs	6-17
6.5.1	Call Signs for Aeronautical (Ground) Stations	6-17

6.5.2	Aircraft call signs	6-18
6.6	Establishment and Continuation of Communications	6-18
6.7	Transfer of Communications	6-20
6.7.1	Phraseology for transfer of control:	6-21
6.8	Test Procedures	6-21
6.9	Issue of Clearance and Readback Requirements	6-22
CHAPTER 7 General Radar Phraseology		7-1
7.1	Introduction	7-1
7.2	Radar Identification and Vectoring	7-1
7.3	Traffic Information and Avoiding Action	7-1
7.4	Secondary Surveillance Radar (SSR)	7-1
7.5	Radar Vectoring	7-2
7.6	Radar Vectors to Final Approach	7-2
7.7	Surveillance Radar Approach	7-2
7.8	Precision Radar Approach	7-3
CHAPTER 8 Meteorological Information		8-1
8.1	Meteorological Information	8-1
8.1.1	Automatic Terminal Information Service (ATIS)	8-1
8.1.2	VOLMET	8-1
CHAPTER 9 VFR Communication Failure		9-1
9.1	Aircraft Communications Failure	9-1
9.1.1	Receiver failure	9-1
9.1.2	Intentions	9-1
9.1.3	SSR Selection and Visual Signals	9-1
CHAPTER 10 Distress and Urgency Procedures		10-1
10.1	Introduction	10-1
10.1.1	General Procedures	10-1
10.1.2	Action by an aircraft in DISTRESS	10-1
10.1.3	Actions by the first station acknowledging the distress message	10-2
10.1.4	Imposition of silence	10-2
10.1.5	Action by all other stations	10-3
10.1.6	Termination of distress communications and of silence	10-3
10.1.7	Action by an aircraft reporting an URGENCY condition	10-4
10.1.8	Actions by the first station acknowledging the urgency message	10-5
CHAPTER 11 Basic Radio Principles		11-1
11.1	Introduction	11-1
11.1.1	Transformer Analogy	11-1
11.1.2	Basic Concept	11-1
11.1.3	Antenna Radiation	11-1
11.1.4	Frequency	11-2
11.2	The Radio Wave	11-2
11.2.1	Wavelength	11-2
11.2.2	Propagation and Attenuation	11-3
11.2.3	Radio Transmission Ranges	11-3
11.2.4	Ground Waves and Sky Waves	11-3
11.2.5	Reflection and Refraction	11-4
11.3	Frequency Bands	11-4
11.3.1	Low Frequency (LF)	11-5
11.3.2	Medium Frequency (MF)	11-5
11.3.3	High Frequency (HF)	11-5
11.3.4	Very High Frequency (VHF)	11-5
11.3.5	Ultra High Frequencies (UHF)	11-6

CRANFIELD AVIATION TRAINING SCHOOL LTD. PART-FCL ATO N° 0136
CATS INNOVATION CENTRE, LUTON, Bedfordshire LU2 8DL U.K.   www.catsaviation.com
ii   Communications

CATS

11.3.6	Super High Frequency (SHF)	11-6
CHAPTER 12 General Operating Procedures		12-1
12.1	Introduction	12-1
12.2	Standard Phraseology	12-1
12.2.1	Pushback	12-1
12.2.2	Flight Plans	12-2
12.2.3	IFR Departures	12-3
12.2.4	IFR Arrivals	12-3
12.2.5	Position Reporting	12-4
12.3	Aircraft Call Signs	12-5
12.4	Vertical Position	12-5
12.5	Level Instructions	12-6
CHAPTER 13 IFR Communication Failure		13-1
13.1	Introduction	13-1
CHAPTER 14 PAN Medical Procedure		14-1
14.1	Aircraft used for medical transports	14-1
CHAPTER 15 Meteorological Information		15-1
15.1	Runway Visual Range	15-1
15.2	Braking Action	15-1
15.3	Aircraft Observations and Reports	15-1
15.3.1	Aircraft Routine Meteorological Observations	15-1
15.3.2	Aircraft Special Meteorological Observations	15-2
15.3.3	Observations made during climb out or approach	15-2
15.3.4	Reporting Procedures	15-2
15.3.5	AIREP messages	15-2
INDEX		i

Introduction

Radiotelephony (RT) provides the means by which pilots and personnel on ground communicate with each other. Used properly, the information and instructions transmitted are of vital importance in assisting in the safe and expeditious operation of aircraft. The use of non-standard procedures and phraseology can cause misunderstanding. Incidents and accidents have occurred in which a contributing factor has been the misunderstanding caused by the use of poor phraseology. The importance of using correct and precise standard phraseology cannot be overemphasised.

The layout of the book

EASA PART-FCL lists theoretical knowledge requirements for communications. At ATPL level the subject is divided into two examinations: VFR and IFR communications. At CPL level only VFR communications is examined and at IR level only IFR communications is examined. Many of the topics covered in VFR communications are also found in IFR communications. This study guide covers both VFR and IFR communications. While the procedures and phraseology specifically reflect the situation in an environment where very high frequency (VHF) is in use they are equally applicable in those areas where high frequency (HF) is used.

Section 1 of this study guide covers VFR communications and Section 2 covers additional information needed for IFR communications.

How to Study VFR Communications

We recommend that you focus on the topics in Section 1 when studying for the VFR communications examination.

How to Study IFR Communications

Subjects in Section 2 should be studied in detail and the rest of the book should be reviewed when studying for the IFR communications examination.

THEORETICAL KNOWLEDGE SYLLABUS AND LEARNING OBJECTIVES

Subject	090 – Communications	Aeroplane		Helicopter			IR
Syllabus reference	Syllabus details and associated Learning Objectives	ATPL	CPL	ATPL/IR	ATPL	CPL	
090 00 00 00	**COMMUNICATIONS**						
091 00 00 00	**VFR COMMUNICATIONS**						
091 01 00 00	**DEFINITIONS**						
091 01 01 00	**Meanings and significance of associated terms**	X	X	X	X	X	
LO	Stations						
LO	Communication methods						
091 01 02 00	**Air Traffic Services abbreviations**	X	X	X	X	X	
LO	Define commonly used Air Traffic Control abbreviations: - Flight conditions - Airspace - Services - Time - Miscellaneous						
091 01 03 00	**Q-code groups commonly used in RTF air-ground communications**	X	X	X	X	X	
LO	Define Q-code groups commonly used in RTF air to ground communications: - Pressure settings - Directions and bearings						
LO	State the procedure for obtaining bearing information in flight						
091 01 04 00	**Categories of messages**	X	X	X	X	X	
LO	List the categories of messages in order of priority						
LO	Identify the types of messages appropriate to each category						
LO	List the priority of a message (given examples of messages to compare)						
091 02 00 00	**GENERAL OPERATING PROCEDURES**						
091 02 01 00	**Transmission of letters**	X	X	X	X	X	
LO	State the phonetic alphabet used in radiotelephony						
LO	Identify the occasions when words should be spelt						
091 02 02 00	**Transmission of numbers (including level information)**	X	X	X	X	X	
LO	Describe the method of transmisssion of numbers: - Pronunciation - Single digits, whole hundreds and whole thousands						
091 02 03 00	**Transmission of time**	X	X	X	X	X	
LO	Describe the ways of transmitting time - Standard time reference (UTC) - Minutes, minutes and hours, when required						
091 02 04 00	**Transmission technique**	X	X	X	X	X	
LO	Explain the techniques used for making good R/T transmissions						
091 02 05 00	**Standard words and phrases (relevant RTF phraseology included)**	X	X	X	X	X	
LO	Define the meaning of standard words and phrases						

CRANFIELD AVIATION TRAINING SCHOOL LTD. PART-FCL ATO N° 0136
CATS INNOVATION CENTRE, LUTON, Bedfordshire LU2 8DL U.K.   www.catsaviation.com

v   Communications

Subject	090 – Communications	Aeroplane		Helicopter			IR
Syllabus reference	Syllabus details and associated Learning Objectives	ATPL	CPL	ATPL/IR	ATPL	CPL	
LO	Use correct phraseology for each phase of VFR flight						
LO	Aerodrome procedures						
	- Departure information						
	- Taxi instructions						
	- Aerodrome traffic and circuits						
	- Final approach and landing						
	- After landing						
	- Essential aerodrome information						
LO	VFR Departure						
LO	VFR Arrival						
091 02 06 00	**Radiotelephony call signs for aeronautical stations including use of abbreviated call signs**	x	x	x	x	x	
LO	Name the two parts of the call sign of an aeronautical station						
LO	Identify the call sign suffixes for aeronautical stations						
LO	Explain when the call sign may be omitted or abbreviated to the use of suffix only						
091 02 07 00	**Radiotelephony call signs for aircraft including use of abbreviated call signs**	x	x	x	x	x	
LO	List the three different ways to compose an aircraft call sign						
LO	Describe the abbreviated forms for aircraft call signs						
LO	Explain when aircraft call signs may be abbreviated						
091 02 08 00	**Transfer of communication**	x	x	x	x	x	
LO	Describe the procedure for transfer of communication						
	- By groundstation						
	- By aircraft						
091 02 09 00	**Test procedures including readability scale**	x	x	x	x	x	
LO	Explain how to test radio transmission and reception						
LO	State the readability scale and explain its meaning						
091 02 10 00	**Read back and acknowledgement requirements**	x	x	x	x	x	
LO	State the requirement to read back ATC route clearances						
LO	State the requirement to read back clearances related to in runway in use						
LO	State the requirement to read back other cleareances including conditional clearances						
LO	State the the requirement to read back other data such as runway, SSR codes etc						
091 02 11 00	**Radar procedural phraseology**	x	x	x	x	x	
LO	Use the correct phraseology for an aircraft receiving a radar service						
	- Radar identification						
	- Radar vectoring						
	- Traffic information and avoidance						
	- SSR procedures						
091 03 00 00	**RELEVANT WEATHER INFORMATION TERMS (VFR)**						
091 03 01 00	**Aerodrome weather**	x	x	x	x	x	

CRANFIELD AVIATION TRAINING SCHOOL LTD. PART-FCL ATO N° 0136
CATS INNOVATION CENTRE, LUTON, Bedfordshire LU2 8DL U.K.   www.catsaviation.com

CATS

vi   Communications

Subject	090 – Communications	Aeroplane		Helicopter			IR
Syllabus reference	Syllabus details and associated Learning Objectives	ATPL	CPL	ATPL/IR	ATPL	CPL	
LO	List the contents of aerodrome weather reports and state units of measurement used for each item - Wind direction and speed - Variation of wind direction and speed - Visibility - Present weather - Cloud amount and type (including the meaning of CAVOK) - Air temperature and dewpoint - Pressure values (QNH, QFE) - Supplementary information (aerodrome warnings, landing runway, runway conditions, restrictions, obstructions, windshear warnings, etc)						
091 03 02 00	**Weather broadcast**	x	x	x	x	x	
LO	List the sources of weather information available for aircraft in flight						
LO	Explain the meaning of the abbreviations: ATIS, VOLMET						
091 04 00 00	**ACTION REQUIRED TO BE TAKEN IN CASE OF COMMUNICATION FAILURE**	x	x	x	x	x	
LO	State the action to be taken in case of communication failure on a controlled VFR-flight						
LO	Identify the frequencies to be used in an attempt to establish communication						
LO	State the additional information that should be transmitted, in the event of receiver failure						
LO	Identify the SSR code that may be used to indicate communication failure						
LO	Explain the action to be taken by a pilot with Com failure in the aerodrome traffic pattern at controlled aerodromes						
091 05 00 00	**DISTRESS AND URGENCY PROCEDURES**	x	x	x	x	x	
091 05 01 00	**Distress (definition – frequencies – watch of distress frequencies – distress signal – distress message)**	x	x	x	x	x	
LO	State the DISTRESS procedures						
LO	Define DISTRESS						
LO	Identify the frequencies that should be used by aircraft in DISTRESS						
LO	Specify the emergency SSR codes that may be used by aircraft, and the meaning of the codes						
LO	Describe the action to be taken by the station which receives a DISTRESS message						
LO	Describe the action to be taken by all other stations when a DISTRESS procedure is in progress						
LO	List the content of a DISTRESS signal/message in the correct sequence						
091 05 02 00	**Urgency (definition – frequencies – urgency signal – urgency message)**	X	x	x	x	x	
LO	State the URGENCY procedures						
LO	Define URGENCY						
LO	Identify the frequencies that should be used by aircraft in URGENCY						
LO	Describe the action to be taken by the station which receives an URGENCY message						

Subject	090 – Communications	Aeroplane		Helicopter			IR
Syllabus reference	Syllabus details and associated Learning Objectives	ATPL	CPL	ATPL/IR	ATPL	CPL	
LO	Describe the action to be taken by all other stations when an URGENCY procedure is in progress						
LO	List the content of an URGENCY signal/message in the correct sequence						
091 06 00 00	GENERAL PRINCIPLES OF VHF PROPAGATION AND ALLOCATION OF FREQUENCIES	x	x	x	x	x	
LO	Describe the radio frequency spectrum with particular reference to VHF						
LO	Describe the radio frequency spectrum of the bands into which the radio frequency spectrum is divided						
LO	Identify the frequency range of the VHF band						
LO	Name the band normally used for Aeronautical Mobile Service voice communication						
LO	State the frequency separation allocated between consecutive VHF frequencies						
LO	Describe the propagation characteristics of radio transmissions in the VHF band						
LO	Describe factors which reduce the effective range and quality of radio transmissions						
LO	State which of these factors apply to the VHF band						
LO	Calculate the effective range of VHF transmissions assuming no attenuating factors						
092 00 00 00	IFR COMMUNICATIONS						
092 01 00 00	DEFINITIONS						
092 01 01 00	Meanings and significance of associated terms	x		x			x
LO	As for VFR plus terms used in conjunction with approach and holding procedures						
092 01 02 00	Air Traffic Control abbreviations	x		x			x
LO	As for VFR plus additional IFR related terms						
092 01 03 00	Q-code groups commonly used in RTF air-ground communications	x		x			x
LO	Define Q-code groups commonly used in RTF air to ground communications: - Pressure settings - Directions and bearings						
LO	State the procedure for obtaining a bearing information in flight						
092 01 04 00	Categories of messages	x		x			x
LO	List the categories of messages in order of priority						
LO	Identify the types of messages appropriate to each category						
LO	List the priority of a message (given examples of messages to compare)						
092 02 00 00	GENERAL OPERATING PROCEDURES						
092 02 01 00	Transmission of letters	x		x			x
LO	State the phonetic alphabet used in radiotelephony						
LO	Identify the occasions when words should be spelt						
092 02 02 00	Transmission of numbers (including level information)	x		x			x

Subject	090 – Communications	Aeroplane		Helicopter			IR
Syllabus reference	Syllabus details and associated Learning Objectives	ATPL	CPL	ATPL/IR	ATPL	CPL	
LO	Describe the method of transmitting numbers						
	- Pronunciation						
	- Single digits, whole hundreds and whole thousands						
092 02 03 00	**Transmission of time**	x		x			x
LO	Describe the ways of transmitting time						
	- Standard time reference (UTC)						
	- Minutes, minutes and hours, when required						
092 02 04 00	**Transmission technique**	x		x			x
LO	Explain the techniques used for making good R/T transmissions						
092 02 05 00	**Standard words and phrases (relevant RTF phraseology included)**	x		x			x
LO	Define the meaning of standard words and phrases						
LO	Use correct standard phraseology for each phase of IFR flight						
	- Pushback						
	- IFR depature						
	- Airways clearances						
	- Position reporting						
	- Approach procedures						
	- IFR arrivals						
092 02 06 00	**Radiotelephony call signs for aeronautical stations including use of abbreviated call signs**	x		x			x
LO	As for VFR						
LO	Name the two parts of the call sign of an aeronautical station						
LO	Identify the call sign suffixes for aeronautical stations						
LO	Explain when the call sign may be abbreviated to the use of suffix only						
092 02 07 00	**Radiotelephony call signs for aircraft including use of abbreviated call signs**	x		x			x
LO	As for VFR						
LO	Explain when the suffix "HEAVY" should be used with an aircraft call sign						
LO	Explain the use of the phrase "Change your call sign to . . ."						
LO	Explain the use of of the phrase "Revert to flight plan call sign"						
092 02 08 00	**Transfer of communication**	x		x			x
LO	Describe the procedure for transfer of communication						
	- By ground station						
	- By aircraft						
092 02 09 00	**Test procedures including readability scale; establishment of RTF communication**	x		x			x
LO	Explain how to test radio transmission and reception						
LO	State the readability scale and explain its meaning						
092 02 10 00	**Read back and acknowledgement requirements**	x		x			x
LO	State the requirement to read back ATC route clearances						
LO	State the requirement to read back clearances related to runway in use						

CRANFIELD AVIATION TRAINING SCHOOL LTD. PART-FCL ATO N° 0136
CATS INNOVATION CENTRE, LUTON, Bedfordshire LU2 8DL U.K.

CATS

ix

www.catsaviation.com

Communications

Subject	090 – Communications	Aeroplane		Helicopter			IR
Syllabus reference	Syllabus details and associated Learning Objectives	ATPL	CPL	ATPL/IR	ATPL	CPL	
LO	State the requirement to read back other clearances including conditional clearances						
LO	State the requirement to read back data such as runway, SSR codes etc						
092 02 11 00	**Radar procedural phraseology**	x		x			x
LO	Use the correct phraseology for an aircraft receiving a radar service - Radar identification - Radar vectoring - Traffic information and avoidance - SSR procedures						
092 02 12 00	**Level changes and reports**	x		x			x
LO	Use the correct term to describe vertical position - In relation to flight level (standard pressure setting) - In relation to Altitude (metres/feet on QNH) - In relation to Height (metres/feet on QFE)						
092 03 00 00	**ACTION REQUIRED TO BE TAKEN IN CASE OF COMMUNICATION FAILURE**	x		x			x
LO	Describe the action to be taken in communication failure on a IFR flight						
LO	Describe the action to be taken in case of communication failure on a IFR flight when flying in VMC and the flight will be terminated in VMC						
LO	Describe the action to be taken in case of communication failure on a IFR flight when flying in IMC						
092 04 00 00	**DISTRESS AND URGENCY PROCEDURES**						
092 04 01 00	**PAN medical**	x		x			x
LO	Describe the type of flights to which PAN MEDICAL applies						
LO	List the content of a PAN MEDICAL message in correct sequence						
092 04 02 00	**Distress (definition – frequencies – watch of distress frequencies – distress signal – distress message)**	x		x			x
LO	State the DISTRESS procedures						
LO	Define DISTRESS						
LO	Identify the frequencies that should be used by aircraft in DISTRESS						
LO	Specify the emergency SSR codes that may be used by aircraft, and the meaning of the codes						
LO	Describe the action to be taken by the station which receives a DISTRESS message						
LO	Describe the action to be taken by all other stations when a DISTRESS procedure is in progress	x		x			x
LO	List the content of a DISTRESS message						
092 04 03 00	**Urgency (definition – frequencies – urgency signal – urgency message)**						
LO	State the URGENCY procedures						
LO	Define URGENCY						
LO	Identify the frequencies that should be used by aircraft in URGENCY						

CRANFIELD AVIATION TRAINING SCHOOL LTD. PART-FCL ATO N° 0136
CATS INNOVATION CENTRE, LUTON, Bedfordshire LU2 8DL U.K.   www.catsaviation.com

x   Communications

Subject	090 – Communications	Aeroplane		Helicopter			IR
Syllabus reference	Syllabus details and associated Learning Objectives	ATPL	CPL	ATPL/IR	ATPL	CPL	
LO	Describe the action to be taken by the station which receives an URGENCY message	x		x			x
LO	**Describe the action to be taken by all other stations when an DISTRESS procedure is in progress**						
LO	List the content of an URGENCY signal/message in the correct sequence						
092 05 00 00	**RELEVANT WEATHER INFORMATION TERM**						
092 05 01 00	**Aerodrome weather**	x		x			x
LO	As for VFR plus the following						
LO	Runway visual range						
LO	Braking action (friction coefficient)						
092 05 02 00	**Weather broadcast**	x		x			x
LO	As for VFR plus the following						
LO	Explain when aircraft routine meteorological observations should be made						
LO	Explain when aircraft Special meteorological observations should be made						
092 06 00 00	**GENERAL PRINCIPLES OF VHF PROPAGATION AND ALLOCATION OF FREQUENCIES**	x		x			x
LO	Describe the radio frequency spectrum with particular reference to VHF						
LO	State the names of the bands into which the radio frequency spectrum is divided						
LO	Identify the frequency range of the VHF band						
LO	Name the band normally used for Aeronautical Mobile Service voice communications						
LO	State the frequency separation allocated between consecutive VHF frequencies						
LO	Describe the propagation characteristics of radio transmissions in the VHF band						
LO	Describe the factors which reduce the effective range and quality of radio transmissions						
LO	State which of these factors apply to the VHF band						
LO	Calculate the effective range of VHF transmissions assuming no attenuating factors						
092 07 00 00	**MORSE CODE**	x	x	x	x	x	x
LO	Identify radio navigation aids (VOR, DME, NDB, ILS) from their morse code identifiers						
LO	SELCAL, TCAS, ACARS phraseology and procedures						

CRANFIELD AVIATION TRAINING SCHOOL LTD. PART-FCL ATO N° 0136
CATS INNOVATION CENTRE, LUTON, Bedfordshire LU2 8DL U.K.   www.catsaviation.com

CATS

xi   Communications

Section 1
VFR Communications

CRANFIELD AVIATION TRAINING SCHOOL LTD. PART-FCL ATO N° 0136
CATS INNOVATION CENTRE, LUTON, Bedfordshire LU2 8DL U.K.

www.catsaviation.com

Communications

CHAPTER 1
Definitions and Abbreviations

1.1   Stations

Aerodrome control radio station
A station providing radio communication between an aerodrome control tower and aircraft or mobile aeronautical stations.

Aeronautical station
A land station in the aeronautical mobile service. In certain instances, an aeronautical station may be located, for example, on board ship or on a platform at sea.

1.2   Communication Methods

Air-ground communication
Two-way communication between aircraft and stations or locations on the surface of the Earth.

Air to ground communication
One-way communication from aircraft to stations or locations on the surface of the Earth.

Blind transmission
A transmission from one station to another station in circumstances where two-way communication cannot be established but where it is believed that the called station is able to receive the transmission.

Broadcast
A transmission of information relating to air navigation that is not addressed to a specific station or stations.

Readback
A procedure whereby the receiving station repeats a received message or appropriate part thereof back to the transmitting station so as to obtain confirmation of correct reception.

Telecommunication
Any transmission, emission or reception of signs, signals, writing, images and sounds or intelligence of any nature by wire, radio, optical or other electromagnetic systems.

1.3   Miscellaneous Definitions

Aerodrome control service
Air traffic control service for aerodrome traffic.

Aerodrome traffic
All traffic on the manoeuvring area of an aerodrome and all aircraft flying in the vicinity of an aerodrome.
Note: an aircraft is in the vicinity of an aerodrome when it is in, entering or leaving an aerodrome traffic circuit.

Aerodrome traffic circuit
The specified path to be flown by aircraft operating in the vicinity of an aerodrome.

Aeronautical fixed service
A telecommunication service between specified fixed points provided primarily for the safety of air navigation and for the regular, efficient and economical operation of air services.

Aeronautical fixed telecommunication network (AFTN)
A world-wide system of aeronautical fixed circuits provided, as part of the aeronautical fixed service, for the exchange of messages and / or digital data between aeronautical fixed stations having the same or compatible communications characteristics.

Aeronautical mobile service
A mobile service between aeronautical stations and aircraft stations, or between aircraft stations, in which survival craft stations may participate; emergency position-indicating radio beacon stations may also participate in this service on designated distress and emergency frequencies.

Aerodrome traffic
All traffic on the manoeuvring area of an aerodrome and all aircraft flying in the vicinity of an aerodrome
Note: An aircraft is in the vicinity of an aerodrome when it is in, entering or leaving an aerodrome traffic circuit.

Air traffic
All aircraft in flight or operating on the manoeuvring area of an aerodrome.

Air traffic control clearance
Authorisation for an aircraft to proceed under conditions specified by an air traffic control unit.

Air traffic service
A generic term meaning variously, flight information service, alerting service, air traffic advisory service, air traffic control service, area control service, approach control service or aerodrome control service.

Air traffic services unit
A generic term meaning variously, air traffic control unit, flight information centre or air traffic services reporting office.

Airway
A control area or portion thereof established in the form of a corridor equipped with radio navigational aids.

Altitude
The vertical distance of a level, a point or an object considered as a point, measured from mean sea level.

Approach control service
Air traffic control service for arriving or departing controlled flights.

Apron
A defined area, on a land aerodrome, intended to accommodate aircraft for purposes of loading or unloading passengers, mail or cargo, fuelling, parking or maintenance.

Area control centre
A unit established to provide air traffic control service to controlled flights in control areas under its jurisdiction.

Automatic terminal information service (ATIS)
The automatic provision of current, routine information, to arriving and departing aircraft throughout 24 h or a specified portion thereof.
Data link-automatic terminal information service (D-ATIS). The provision of ATIS via a data link.

Voice-automatic terminal information service (Voice-ATIS). The provision of ATIS by means of continuous and repetitive voice broadcasts.

Clearance limit
The point to which an aircraft is granted an air traffic control clearance.

Controlled airspace
An airspace of defined dimensions within which air traffic control service is provided in accordance with the airspace classification.
Note: Controlled airspace is a generic term which covers A, B, C, D, and E.

Control zone
A controlled airspace extending upwards from the surface of the earth to a specified upper limit.

Expected approach time
The time at which ATC expects that an arriving aircraft, following a delay, will leave the holding point to complete its approach for a landing.

Flight information centre
A unit established to provide flight information service and alerting service.

Flight level
A surface of constant atmospheric pressure which is related to a specific pressure datum, 1013.25 hPa, and is separated from other such surfaces by specific pressure intervals.
Note: A pressure type altimeter calibrated in accordance with the Standard Atmosphere:
- when set to a QNH altimeter setting, will indicate altitude;
- when set to QFE altimeter setting, will indicate height above the QFE reference datum:
- when set to a pressure of 1013.25 hPa, may be used to indicate flight levels.

Flight plan
Specified information provided to air traffic services units, relative to an intended flight or portions of a flight of an aircraft.

Heading
The direction in which the longitudinal axis of an aircraft is pointed, usually expressed in degrees from North (true, magnetic, compass or grid).

Holding fix
A geographical location that serves as a reference for a holding procedure.

Holding procedure
A predetermined manoeuvre which keeps an aircraft within a specified airspace while awaiting further clearance.

IFR flight
A flight conducted in accordance with the instrument flight rules.

Instrument meteorological conditions
Meteorological conditions expressed in terms of visibility, distance from cloud, and ceiling, less than the minima specified for visual meteorological conditions.

Level

A generic term relating to the vertical position of an aircraft in flight and meaning variously, height, altitude or flight level.

Manoeuvring area
That part of an aerodrome to be used for the take-off, landing and taxiing of aircraft, excluding aprons.

Missed approach procedure
The procedure to be followed if the approach cannot be continued.

Movement area
That part of an aerodrome to be used for the take-off, landing and taxiing of aircraft, consisting of the manoeuvring area and the apron(s).

Radar approach
An approach, executed by an aircraft, under the direction of a radar controller.

Radar identification
The situation which exists when the radar position of a particular aircraft is seen on a radar display and positively identified by an air traffic controller.

Radar vectoring
Provision of navigational guidance to aircraft in the form of specific headings, based on the use of radar.

Reporting point
A specified geographical location in relation to which the position of an aircraft can be reported.

Runway visual range
The range over which the pilot of an aircraft on the centre line of a runway, can see the runway surface markings or the lights delineating the runway or identifying its centre line.

Touchdown
The point where the nominal glide path intercepts the runway.

Track
The projection on the earth's surface of the path of an aircraft, the direction of which path at any point is usually expressed in degrees from North (true, magnetic or grid).

VFR flight
A flight conducted in accordance with the visual flight rules.

Visual approach
An approach by an IFR flight when either part or all of an instrument approach procedure is not completed and the approach is executed in visual reference to terrain.

Visual meteorological conditions
Meteorological conditions expressed in terms of visibility, distance from cloud, and ceiling, equal to or better than specified minima.

1.4   Air Traffic Control Abbreviations

The abbreviations listed below are normally spoken using the constituent letters, rather than the spelling alphabet, except that those indicated by an asterisk(*) are normally spoken as complete words.

AAL	Above airport level
ACC	Area control centre or area control
ADF	Automatic direction-finding equipment
ADR	Advisory route
AFIS	Aerodrome flight information service
AGL	Above ground level
AIP	Aeronautical information publication
AIRAC*	Aeronautical information regulation and control
AIS	Aeronautical information services
AMSL	Above mean sea level
ATC	Air traffic control (in general)
ATD	Actual time of departure
ATIS*	Automatic terminal information service
ATS	Air traffic services
ATZ	Aerodrome traffic zone
CAVOK*	(Ceiling and Visibility OK) Visibility, cloud and present weather better than prescribed values or conditions
CTR	Control zone
DME	Distance measuring equipment
EET	Estimated elapsed time
ETA	Estimated time of arrival or estimating arrival
ETD	Estimated time of departure or estimating departure
FIC	Flight information centre
FIR	Flight information region
FIS	Flight information service
GCA	Ground controlled approach system or ground controlled approach
H24	Continuous day and night service
HF	High frequency (3 to 30 MHz)
HN	Sunset to sunrise
HJ	Sunrise to sunset
IFR	Instrument flight rules
ILS	Instrument landing system
IMC	Instrument meteorological conditions
INFO*	Information
INS	Inertial navigation system
LORAN	LORAN (long-range air navigation system)
MET*	Meteorological or meteorology
METAR	Meteorological Aerodrome Report
MLS	Microwave landing system
MNPS	Minimum navigation performance specifications
NDB	Non-directional radio beacon
NIL*	None or I have nothing to send you
NOTAM*	A notice containing information concerning the establishment, condition or change in any aeronautical facility, service, procedure or hazard, the timely knowledge of which is essential to personnel concerned with flight operations
PAPI	Precision Approach Path Indicator
QFE	Atmospheric pressure at aerodrome elevation (or at runway threshold)
QNH	Altimeter sub-scale setting to obtain elevation when on the ground
RCC	Rescue co-ordination centre
RNAV*	Area navigation
RVR	Runway visual range
SELCAL*	A system which permits the selective calling of individual aircraft over radiotelephone

	channels linking a ground station with the aircraft
SID	Standard instrument departure
SIGMET*	Information concerning en-route operations weather phenomena which may affect the safety of aircraft
SNOWTAM*	A special series NOTAM notifying the presence or removal of hazardous conditions due to snow, ice, slush or standing water associated with snow, slush and ice on the movement area, by means of a specific format
SPECIAL*	Special meteorological report (in abbreviated plain language)
SSR	Secondary surveillance radar
SST	Supersonic transport
STAR*	Standard (instrument) arrival
TACAN*	UHF tactical air navigation aid
TAF*	Aerodrome forecast
TMA	Terminal control area
UHF	Ultra-high frequency (300 to 3 000 MHz)
UIR	Upper flight information region
UTA	Upper control area
UTC	Co-ordinated universal time
VASIS*	Visual approach slope indicator system
VFR	Visual flight rules
VHF	Very high frequency
VDF	Very high frequency direction-finding station (30 to 300 MHz)
VIP	Very important person
VMC	Visual meteorological conditions
VOLMET*	Meteorological information for aircraft in flight
VOR	VHF omni directional radio range
VORTAC	VOR and TACAN combination

CHAPTER 2
Communication Systems

2.1   General

The most common communication system in use is the Very High Frequency (VHF) system. In addition, large aircraft are usually equipped with (High Frequency) HF communication systems. Airborne communications systems vary considerably in size, weight, power requirements, quality of operation, and cost, depending upon the desired operation. Modern airborne VHF and HF communication systems use transceivers. A transceiver is a self-contained transmitter and receiver that share common circuits: i.e., power supply, antenna and tuning. The transmitter and receiver both operate on the same frequency and the microphone button determines when there is an output from the transmitter. In the absence of transmission, the receiver is sensitive to incoming signals. Since weight and space are of great importance in aircraft, the transceiver is widely used. Large aircraft may be equipped with transceivers or a communications system that use separate transmitters and receivers.

2.1.1   Operation

The operation of radio equipment is essentially the same, whether installed on large aircraft or small aircraft. In some radio installations, the controls for frequency selection, volume, and the "on / off" switch are integral with the radio main chassis. In other installations, the controls are mounted on a panel located in the cockpit and the radio equipment is located in racks in another part of the aircraft.

2.2   Aeronautical Mobile Service

2.2.1   Definition

The Aeronautical Mobile Service is defined as communication between aeronautical stations and aircraft stations, or between aircraft stations, in which survival craft stations may participate and emergency position-indicating radio beacon stations may also participate on designated distress and emergency frequencies. ICAO describes the rules for using the aeronautical mobile network in ICAO Annex 10 Volume 2.

2.2.2   Radio Communication Discipline

In all communications, the highest standard of discipline shall be observed at all times. In all situations for which standard radiotelephony phraseology is specified, it shall be used. The transmission of messages on aeronautical mobile frequencies, when the aeronautical fixed services are able to serve the intended purpose, shall be avoided. The consequences of human performance can affect the understanding of messages and should be taken into consideration. Except as otherwise provided, the responsibility of establishing communication shall rest with the station having traffic to transmit.

> After a call has been made to the aeronautical station, a period of at least 10 s should elapse before a second call is made

Allowing 10 s between radiotelephony calls should eliminate unnecessary transmissions while the aeronautical station is getting ready to reply to the initial call. When an aeronautical station is called simultaneously by several aircraft stations, the aeronautical station shall decide the order in which aircraft shall communicate.

2.2.3 Duration of Communication

In communications between aircraft stations, the duration of communication shall be controlled by the aircraft station which is receiving, subject to the intervention of an aeronautical station. If such communications take place on an ATS frequency, prior permission of the aeronautical station shall be obtained. Such request for permission is not required for brief exchanges.

CHAPTER 3
Q-Codes

3.1 Request for service

For use in radiotelephony, a number of Q-codes have been established. They are coded abbreviations; their purpose is to shorten the duration of radiotelephony messages. They are used when requesting bearings, headings, positions and barometric pressure. To request such information, the aircraft shall call the aeronautical station or the direction finding control station and specify the type of service that is desired by the use of the appropriate phrase or Q signal.

3.2 Common Q-Codes

3.2.1 Pressure Settings

QNH the pressure at the airport reduced to sea level with regard to standard atmospheric conditions.
QFE when altimeter is set to QFE altimeter setting, it will indicate height above the QFE reference datum.

3.2.2 Directions and bearings

QDM	magnetic heading to steer with no wind, to make for the direction-finding station or other specified point
QDR	magnetic bearing of the aircraft from the direction-finding station or point
QTE	true bearing of the aircraft in relation to the direction-finding station or other specified point
QUJ	true heading to be steered by the aircraft, with no wind, to head for the direction-finding station

QGE distance from the direction-finding station or point.
QGH a ground interpreted let down procedure using direction finding equipment
QTF position in relation to a point of reference or in latitude and longitude
QDL An aircraft station requiring a series of bearings or headings, shall call the direction-finding station concerned, on the appropriate frequency, and request the service by the signal QDL followed by other appropriate Q signals.

An aircraft station that requests a bearing shall end the transmission by repeating its call sign. If the transmission has been too short for the direction-finding station to obtain a bearing, the aircraft shall give a longer transmission for two periods of approximately ten seconds.

The direction-finding station shall advise the aircraft station of the heading or bearing in the following form:

- the appropriate phrase or Q signal
- bearing or heading in degrees in relation to the direction-finding station, sent as three figures
- class of bearing (except in QDL procedure)
- time of observation, if necessary (except in QDL procedure).

As soon as the aircraft station has received the bearing, heading or position, it shall repeat back the message for confirmation, or correction, except in QDL procedure.

3.2.3 Accuracy of Bearings and Positions

According to the estimate by the direction-finding station of the accuracy of the observations, bearings and positions shall be classified as follows:

3.2.3.1 Bearings

Class A - accurate within ± 2°
Class B - accurate within ± 5°
Class C - accurate within ± 10°
Class D - accuracy less than Class C

3.2.3.2 Positions

Class A - accurate within 9.3 km (5 NM)
Class B - accurate within 37 km (20 NM)
Class C - accurate within 92 km (50 NM)
Class D - accuracy less than Class C

CHAPTER 4
Categories of Messages

4.1   Priority of messages

The categories of messages handled by the aeronautical mobile service and the order of priority in the establishment of communications and the transmission of messages shall be in accordance with the following table.

Message category and order of priority	Radiotelephony signal
1. Distress calls, distress messages and distress traffic	MAYDAY
2. Urgency messages, including messages preceded by the medical transports signal	PAN, PAN *or* PAN, PAN MEDICAL
3. Communications relating to direction finding	
4. Flight safety messages	
5. Meteorological messages	
6. Flight regularity messages	

4.1.1   Distress Messages

Distress messages and distress traffic shall be handled in accordance with the provisions of *CHAPTER 10, Distress and Urgency Procedures*.

4.1.2   Urgency Messages

Urgency messages and urgency traffic, including messages preceded by the medical transports signal, shall be handled in accordance with the provisions of *CHAPTER 10, Distress and Urgency Procedures*.
Note - The term "medical transports" refers to any means of transportation by land, water, or air; whether military or civilian, permanent or temporary, assigned exclusively to medical transportation and under the control of a competent authority of a party to the conflict.

4.1.3   Direction Finding

Communications relating to direction finding shall be handled in accordance with the procedures outlined in *CHAPTER 3, Q-Codes*.

4.1.4   Flight Safety Messages

Flight safety messages shall comprise the following:
1. movement and control messages;
2. messages originated by an aircraft operating agency or by an aircraft, of immediate concern to an aircraft in flight;
3. meteorological advice of immediate concern to an aircraft in flight or about to depart (individually communicated or for broadcast);
4. other messages concerning aircraft in flight or about to depart.

4.1.5 Meteorological Messages

Meteorological messages shall comprise meteorological information to or from aircraft, other than those listed above.

4.1.6 Flight Regularity Messages

Flight regularity messages shall comprise the following:

1. messages regarding the operation or maintenance of facilities essential for the safety or regularity of aircraft operation
2. messages concerning the servicing of aircraft
3. instructions to aircraft operating agency representatives concerning changes in requirements for passengers and crew caused by unavoidable deviations from normal operating schedules. Individual requirements of passengers or crew shall not be admissible in this type of message
4. messages concerning non-routine landings to be made by the aircraft
5. messages concerning aircraft parts and materials urgently required
6. messages concerning changes in aircraft operating schedules

CHAPTER 5
General Operating Procedures

5.1 Transmission of Letters

When words are spelled out in radiotelephony the phonetic alphabet shown below shall be used. To expedite communications, the use of phonetic spelling should be dispensed with if there is no risk of this affecting correct reception and intelligibility of the message. With the exception of the telephony designator and the type of aircraft, each letter in the aircraft call sign shall be spoken separately using the phonetic spelling.

Letter	Word	Pronunciation *Note: Syllables to emphasise are underlined*	Morse
A	Alpha	AL FAH	• —
B	Bravo	BRAH VOH	— • • •
C	Charlie	CHAR LEE *or* SHAR LEE	— • — •
D	Delta	DELL TAH	— • •
E	Echo	ECK OH	•
F	Foxtrot	FOKS TROT	• • — •
G	Golf	GOLF	— — •
H	Hotel	HOH TELL	• • • •
I	India	IN DEE AH	• •
J	Juliet	JEW LEE ETT	• — — —
K	Kilo	KEY LOH	— • —
L	Lima	LEE MAH	• — — • •
M	Mike	MIKE	— —
N	November	NO VEM BER	— •
O	Oscar	OSS CAH	— — —
P	Papa	PAH PAH	• — — •
Q	Quebec	KEH BECK	— — • —
R	Romeo	ROW ME OH	• — •
S	Sierra	SEE AIR RAH	• • •
T	Tango	TANG GO	—
U	Uniform	YOU NEE FORM *or* OO NEE FORM	• • —
V	Victor	VIK TAH	• • • —
W	Whiskey	WISS KEY	• — —
X	X-ray	ECKS RAY	— • • —
Y	Yankee	YANG KEY	— • — —
Z	Zulu	ZOO LOO	— — • •

5.2 Transmission of Numbers

Numbers shall be transmitted using the following pronunciation.

Number or Numeral Element	Pronunciation
0	ZE-RO
1	WUN
2	TOO
3	TREE
4	FOW-er
5	FIFE
6	SIX
7	SEV-en
8	AIT
9	NIN-er
Decimal	DAY-SEE-MAL
Hundred	HUN-dred
Thousand	TOU-SAND

Note: The syllables printed in capital letters are to be stressed; for example, the two syllables in ZE-RO are given equal emphasis, whereas the first syllable of FOW-er is given primary emphasis.

All numbers except whole hundreds, whole thousands and combinations of thousands and whole hundreds shall be transmitted by pronouncing each digit separately. Whole hundreds and whole thousands shall be transmitted by pronouncing each digit in the number of hundreds or thousands followed by the word HUNDRED or THOUSAND as appropriate. Combinations of thousands and whole hundreds shall be transmitted by pronouncing each digit in the number of thousands followed by the word THOUSAND and the number of hundreds followed by the word HUNDRED.

Number	Transmitted as	Pronounced as
10	ONE ZERO	WUN ZE-RO
75	SEVEN FIVE	SEV-en FIFE
100	ONE HUNDRED	WUN HUN-dred
583	FIVE EIGHT THREE	FIFE AIT TREE
2500	TWO THOUSAND FIVE HUNDRED	TOO TOU-SAND FIFE HUND-dred
5000	FIVE THOUSAND	FIFE THOU-SAND
11000	ONE ONE THOUDSAND	WUN WUN TOU-SAND
25000	TWO FIVE THOUSAND	TOO FIFE TOU-SAND
38143	THREE EIGHT ONE FOUR THREE	TREE AIT WUN FOW-er TREE

Numbers containing a decimal point shall be transmitted with the decimal point in appropriate sequence being indicated by the word DECIMAL.

Number	Transmitted as	Pronounced as
118.1	ONE ONE EIGHT DECIMAL ONE	WUN WUN AIT DAY-SEE-MAL WUN
120.37	ONE TWO ZERO DECIMAL THREE SEVEN	WUN TOO ZE-RO DAY-SEE-MAL TREE SEV-en

CRANFIELD AVIATION TRAINING SCHOOL LTD. PART-FCL ATO N° 0136
CATS INNOVATION CENTRE, LUTON, Bedfordshire LU2 8DL U.K.

www.catsaviation.com

5-2

Communications

5.3   Transmission of Time

When transmitting time, only the minutes of the hour are normally required. However, the hour should be included if there is any possibility of confusion. Co-ordinated Universal Time (UTC) shall be used.

Time	Transmitted as	Pronounced as
0803	ZERO TREE *or*	ZE-RO TREE *or*
	ZERO EIGHT ZERO THREE	ZE-RO AIT ZE-RO TREE
1300	ONE THREE ZERO ZERO	WUN TREE ZE-RO ZE-RO
2057	FIVE SEVEN *or*	FIFE SEV-en *or*
	TWO ZERO FIVE SEVEN	TOO ZE-RO FIFE SEV-en

Pilots may check the time with the appropriate ATS unit. Time checks shall be given to the nearest half-minute.

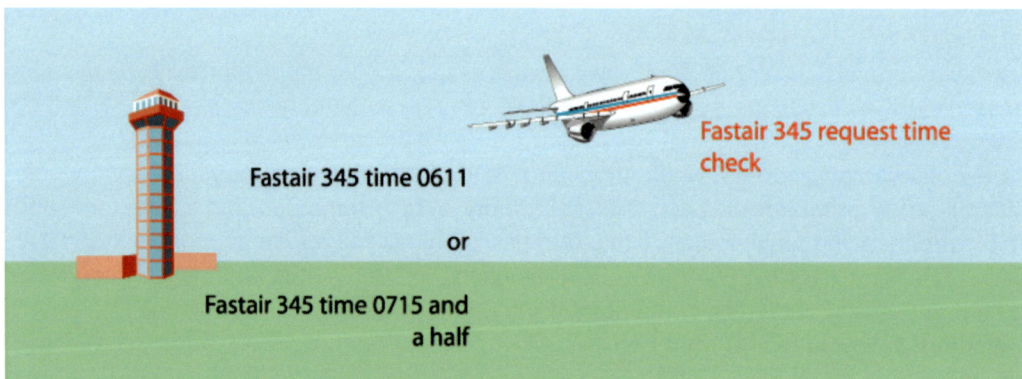

Figure 5.1 Transmission of time

5.4   Transmitting Techniques

The following transmitting techniques will assist in ensuring that transmitted speech is clearly and satisfactorily received:

- Before transmitting, listen out on the frequency to be used to ensure that there will be no interference with a transmission from another station.
- Be familiar with good microphone operating techniques.
- Use a normal conversational tone, speak clearly and distinctly.
- Maintain an even rate of speech not exceeding 100 words per minute. When it is known that the recipient will write down elements of the message, speak at a slightly slower rate.
- Maintain the speaking volume at a constant level.
- A slight pause before and after numbers will assist in making them easier to understand.
- Avoid using hesitation sounds such as "er".
- Depress the transmit switch fully before speaking and do not release it until the message is completed. This will ensure that the entire message is transmitted.

5.4.1   Stuck microphone

An irritating and potentially dangerous situation in radiotelephony is a stuck microphone button. Operators should always ensure that the transmit button is released after a transmission and the microphone is placed in an appropriate place that will ensure that it will not inadvertently be switched on.

CRANFIELD AVIATION TRAINING SCHOOL LTD. PART-FCL ATO N° 0136
CATS INNOVATION CENTRE, LUTON, Bedfordshire LU2 8DL U.K.
www.catsaviation.com
Communications

EASA PART-FCL STUDY GUIDES

VFR & IFR COMMUNICATIONS

CHAPTER 6
Standard Phraseology

6.1 Standard Words and Phrases

Word / Phrase	Meaning
ACKNOWLEDGE	Let me know that you have received and understood this message.
AFFIRM	Yes
APPROVED	Permission for proposed action granted.
BREAK	I hereby indicate the separation between portions of the message. *(To be used where there is no clear distinction between the text and other portions of the message.)*
BREAK BREAK	I hereby indicate the separation between messages transmitted to different aircraft in a very busy environment.
CANCEL	Annul the previously transmitted clearance.
CHECK	Examine a system or procedure. *(No answer is normally expected.)*
CLEARED	Authorised to proceed under the conditions specified.
CONFIRM	Have I correctly received the following . . .? *or* Did you correctly receive this message?
CONTACT	Establish radio contact with . . .
CORRECT	That is correct.
CORRECTION	An error has been made in this transmission (or message indicated). The correct version is . , .
DISREGARD	Consider that transmission as not sent.
GO AHEAD	Proceed with your message. *Note. - The phrase "GO AHEAD" is not normally used in surface movement communications.*
HOW DO YOU READ	What is the readability of my transmission?
I SAY AGAIN	I repeat for clarity or emphasis.
MONITOR	Listen out on (frequency).
NEGATIVE	No *or* Permission not granted *or* That is not correct.
OUT	This exchange of transmissions is ended and no response is expected. *Note.- The word "OUT" is not normally used in VHF communications.*
OVER	My transmission is ended and I expect a response from you. *Note.- The word "OVER" is not normally used in VHF communications.*
READ BACK	Repeat all, or the specified part, of this message back to me exactly as received.
RECLEARED	A change has been made to your last clearance and this new clearance supersedes your previous clearance or part thereof.
REPORT	Pass me the following information.
REQUEST	I should like to know . . ., *or* I wish to obtain . . .
ROGER	I have received all of your last transmission.

	Note.- Under no circumstances to be used in reply to a question requiring "READ BACK" or a direct answer in the affirmative (AFFIRM) or negative (NEGATIVE).
SAY AGAIN	Repeat all, or the following part, of your last transmission.
SPEAK SLOWER	Reduce your rate of speech.
STAND BY	Wait and I will call you.
VERIFY	Check and confirm with originator.
WILCO	(Abbreviation for "will comply".)
	I understand your message and will comply with it.
WORDS TWICE	a) *As a request:* Communication is difficult. Please send every word or group of words twice.
	b) *As information:* Since communication is difficult, every word or group of words in this message will be sent twice

Phraseology details have been established for the purpose of ensuring uniformity in R/T communications. Obviously, it is not practicable to detail phraseology examples suitable for every situation that may occur. However, if standard phrases are adhered to when composing a message, any possible ambiguity will be reduced to a minimum.

Some abbreviations, which by their common usage have become part of aviation terminology, may be spoken using their constituent letters rather than the spelling alphabet, for example, ILS, QNH, RVR, etc.

The following words may be omitted from transmissions provided that no confusion or ambiguity will result:
- "SURFACE" in relation to surface wind direction and speed.
- "DEGREES" in relation to radar headings.
- "VISIBILITY", "CLOUD" and "HEIGHT" in meteorological reports.
- "HECTOPASCALS" when giving pressure settings.

The use of courtesies should be avoided. The word "IMMEDIATELY" should only be used when immediate action is required for safety reasons.

6.2   Aerodrome Procedures

Concise and unambiguous phraseology used at the correct time, is vital to the smooth, safe and expeditious operation of an aerodrome. It is not the only means by which controllers carry out their task, but it also assists pilots in maintaining an awareness of other traffic in their vicinity, particularly in poor visibility conditions. Controllers should not transmit to an aircraft during take-off, the last part of final approach or the landing roll, unless it is necessary for safety reasons, as it may be distracting to the pilot at a time when the cockpit workload is often at its highest.

6.2.1 Departure Information and Engine Starting Procedures

Where no ATIS is provided, the pilot may ask for current aerodrome information before requesting start up.

Georgetown ground Fastair 345, IFR to Colinton, request departure information

Fastair 345 departure runway 32, wind 290 degrees 4 knots QNH 1022, Temperature minus 2, dewpoint minus 3, RVR 550 metres

Runway 32, QNH 1022, will call for start up, Fastair 345

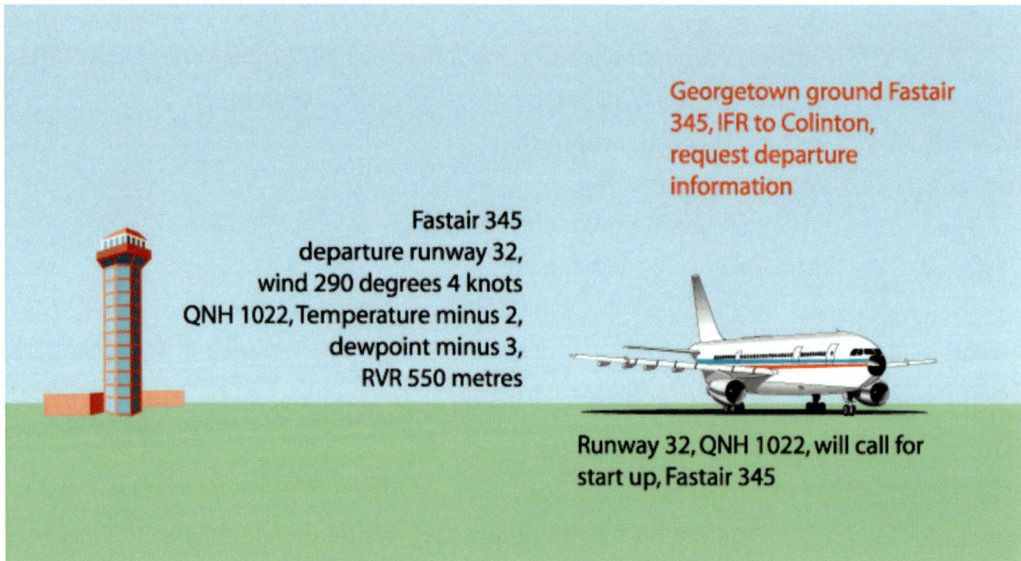

Figure 6.1 Requesting departure information

Requests to start engines are normally made to facilitate ATC planning and to avoid excessive fuel wastage by aircraft delayed on the ground. At certain aerodromes the pilot will state, along with the request, the location of the aircraft and acknowledge receipt of the ATIS broadcast. When there will be a delay to the departure of the aircraft the controller will normally indicate a time to start up or expect to start up.

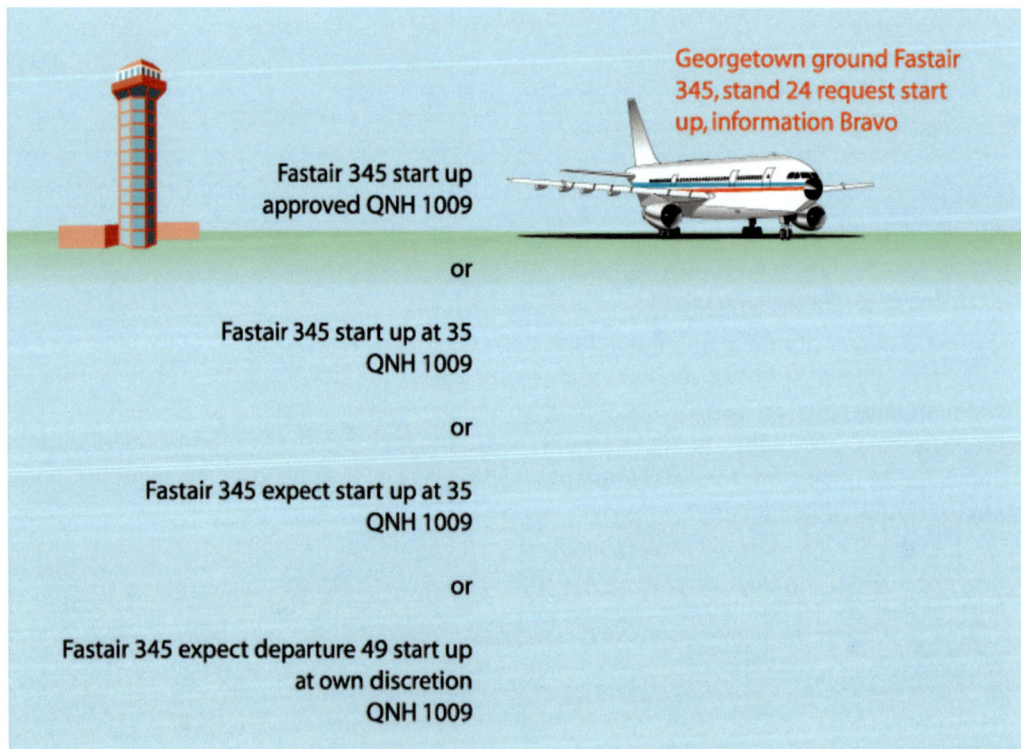

Georgetown ground Fastair 345, stand 24 request start up, information Bravo

Fastair 345 start up approved QNH 1009

or

Fastair 345 start up at 35 QNH 1009

or

Fastair 345 expect start up at 35 QNH 1009

or

Fastair 345 expect departure 49 start up at own discretion QNH 1009

Figure 6.2 Requesting start-up

Having received ATC approval, the pilot starts the engines, assisted as necessary by ground crew.

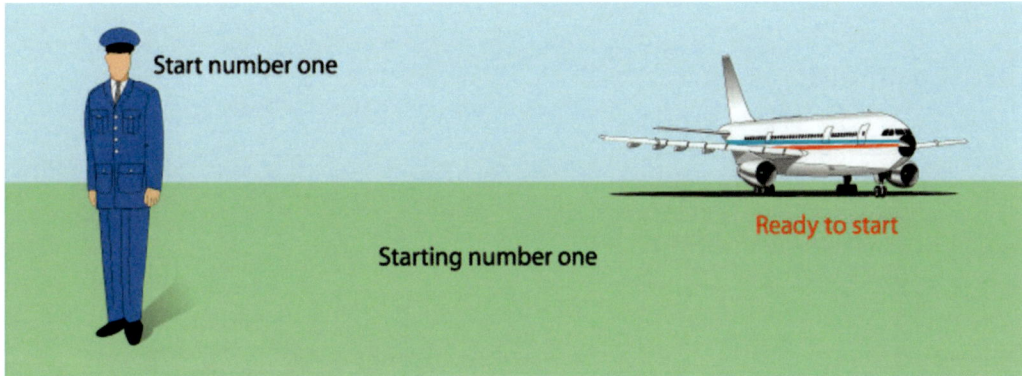

Figure 6.3 Starting engines

6.2.2   Taxi Instructions

Taxi instructions issued by a controller will always contain a clearance limit, which is the point at which the aircraft must stop until further permission to proceed is given. For departing aircraft the clearance limit will normally be the holding point of the runway in use, but it may be any other position on the aerodrome depending on the prevailing traffic circumstances.

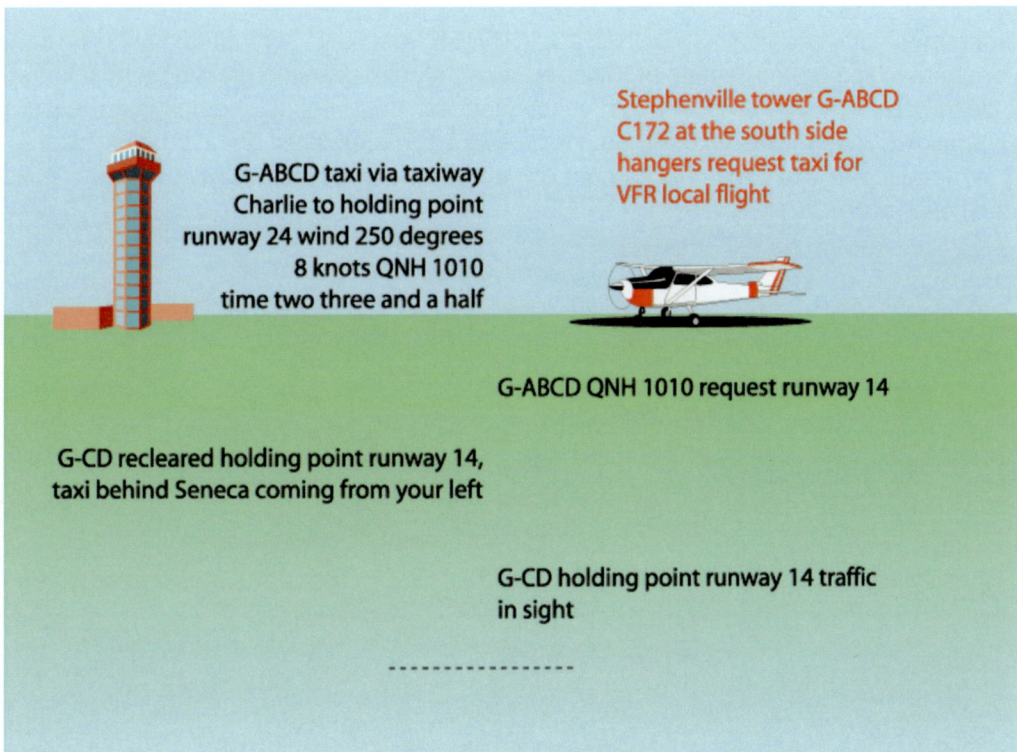

Figure 6.4 Taxi instructions

Where an aircraft acknowledges receipt of the ATIS broadcast, the controller does not need to pass departure information to the pilot when giving taxi instructions.

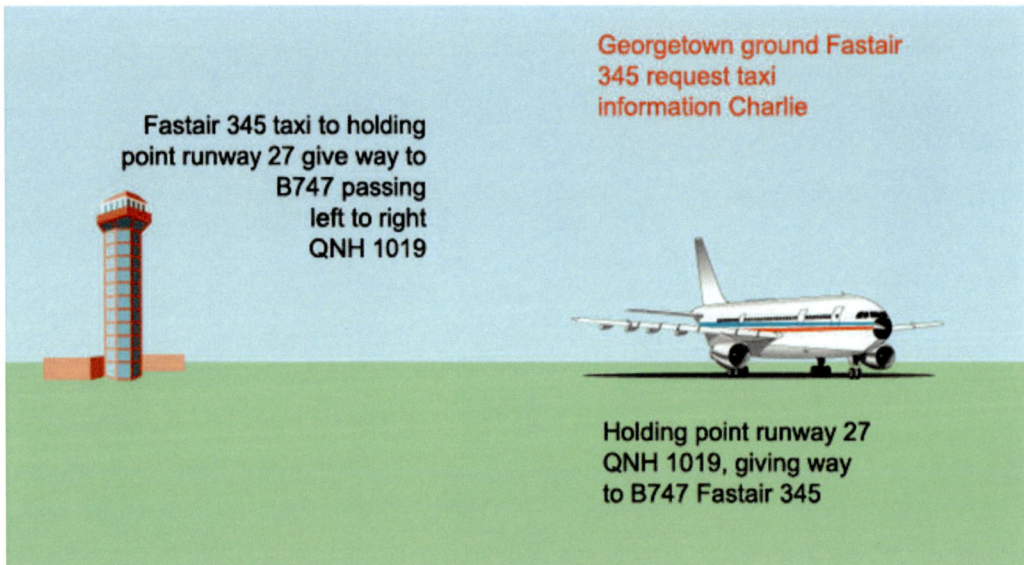

Figure 6.5 Taxi instructions

6.2.3 Take-Off Procedures

At busy aerodromes with separate GROUND and TOWER functions, aircraft are usually transferred to TOWER at or approaching the holding point. Since misunderstandings in the granting and acknowledgement of take-off clearances can result in serious consequences, care should be taken to ensure that the phraseology employed during the taxi manoeuvres cannot be interpreted as a take-off clearance. Some aircraft may be required to carry out checks prior to departure and are not always ready for take-off when they reach the holding point.

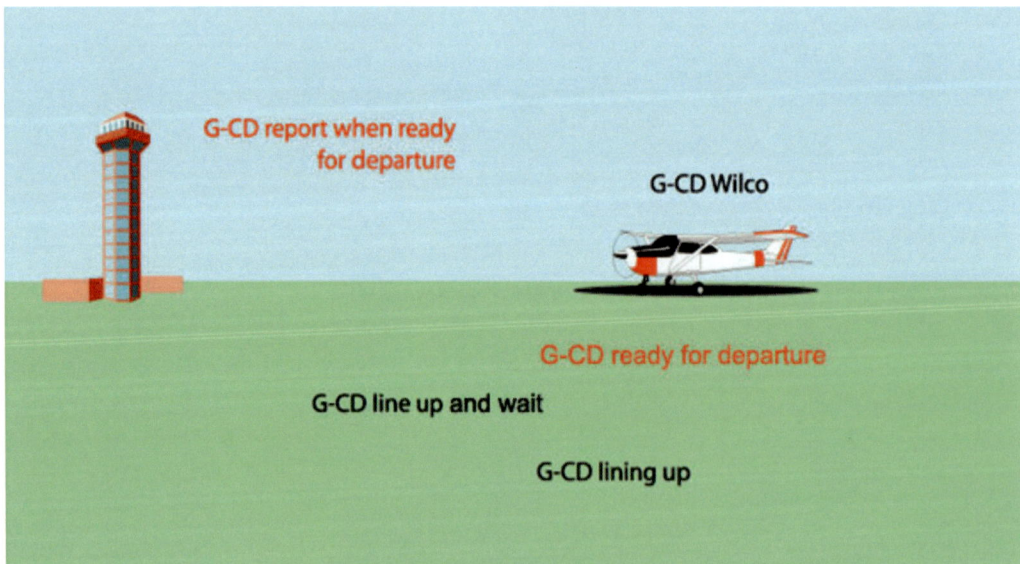

Figure 6.6 Reporting ready for departure

Except in cases of emergency, controllers should not transmit to an aircraft in the process of taking off or during the early stage of climb. For traffic reasons it may be necessary for the aircraft to take off immediately after lining up.

CRANFIELD AVIATION TRAINING SCHOOL LTD. PART-FCL ATO N° 0136
CATS INNOVATION CENTRE, LUTON, Bedfordshire LU2 8DL U.K.   www.catsaviation.com

6-5

Communications

Figure 6.7   Cleared for take-off

Figure 6.8   Immediate take-off

In poor visibility the controller may request the pilot to report when airborne.

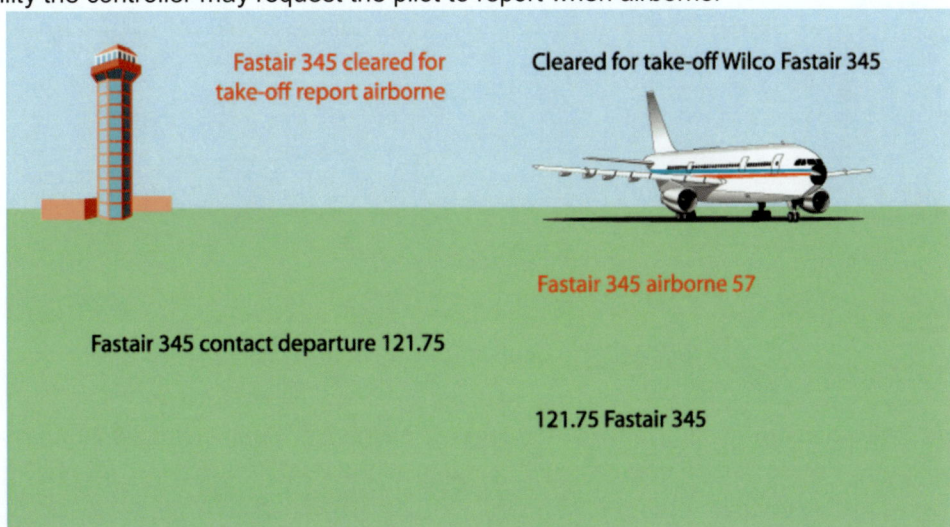

Figure 6.9   Reporting airborne

CRANFIELD AVIATION TRAINING SCHOOL LTD. PART-FCL ATO N° 0136
CATS INNOVATION CENTRE, LUTON, Bedfordshire LU2 8DL U.K.

www.catsaviation.com

6-6

Communications

Conditional clearances shall not be used for movements affecting the active runway(s), except when the aircraft or vehicles concerned are seen by both the controller and pilot. When the conditional clearance involves a departing aircraft and an arriving aircraft it is important that the departing aircraft correctly identifies the arriving aircraft on which the conditional clearance is based. Reference to the arriving aircraft type may be insufficient and it may be necessary to add a description of the colour or the company name to ensure correct identification. A conditional clearance shall be given as follows:

- call sign
- the condition
- the clearance

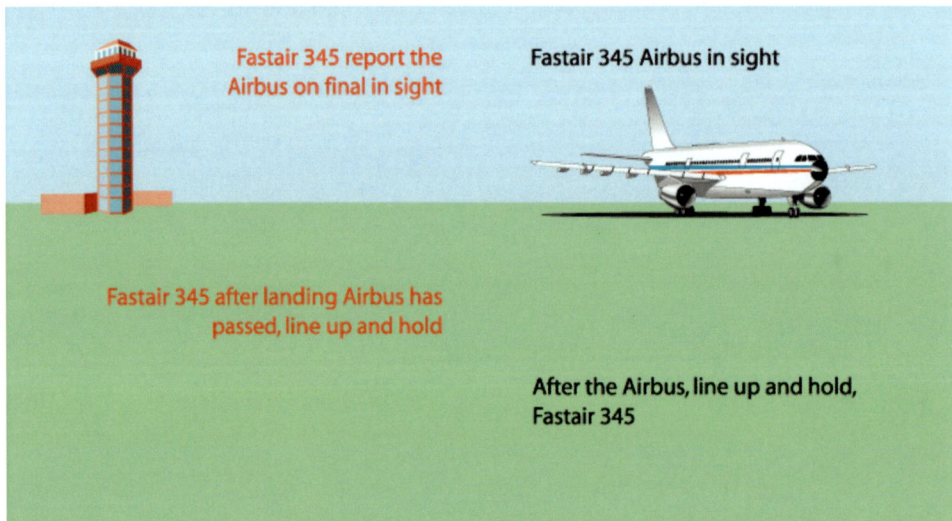

Figure 6.10   Conditional clearances

When several runways are in use and there is any possibility that the pilot may be confused as to which one to use, the runway number should be stated in the take-off clearance.

Figure 6.11   Stating runway numbers

Local departure instructions may be given with the take-off clearance. Such instructions are normally given to ensure separation between aircraft operating in the vicinity of the aerodrome.

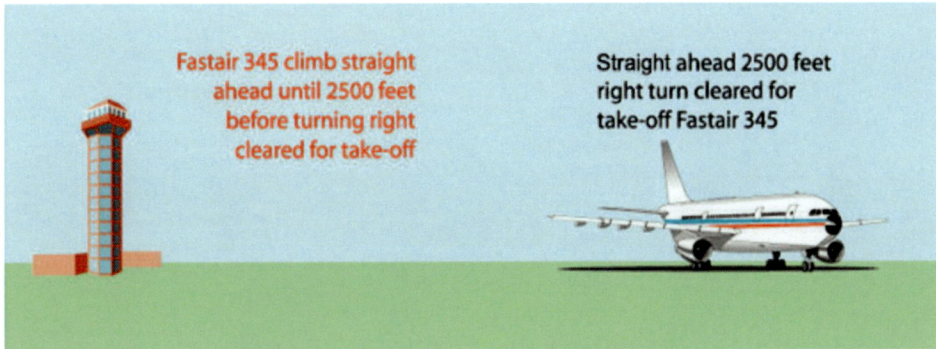

Figure 6.12   Local departure clearances

Due to unexpected traffic developments or a departing aircraft taking longer to take off than anticipated, it is occasionally necessary to cancel the take-off clearance or quickly free the runway for landing traffic.

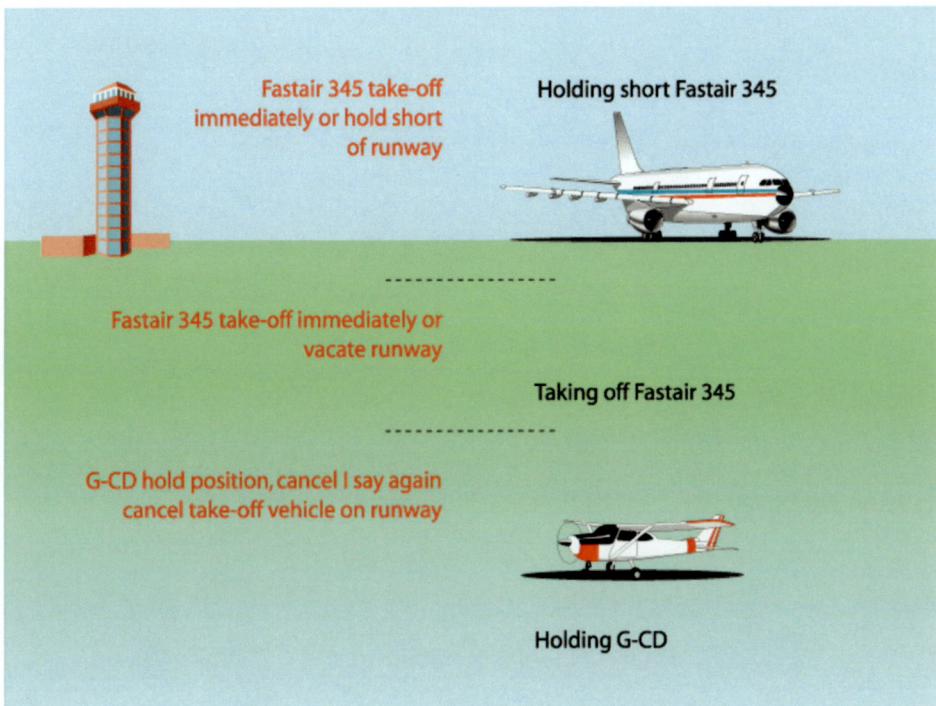

Figure 6.13   Cancelled take-off clearance

When an aircraft has commenced the take-off roll, and it is necessary for the aircraft to abandon take-off, in order to avert a dangerous traffic situation, the aircraft should be instructed to stop immediately and this instruction and call sign, repeated.

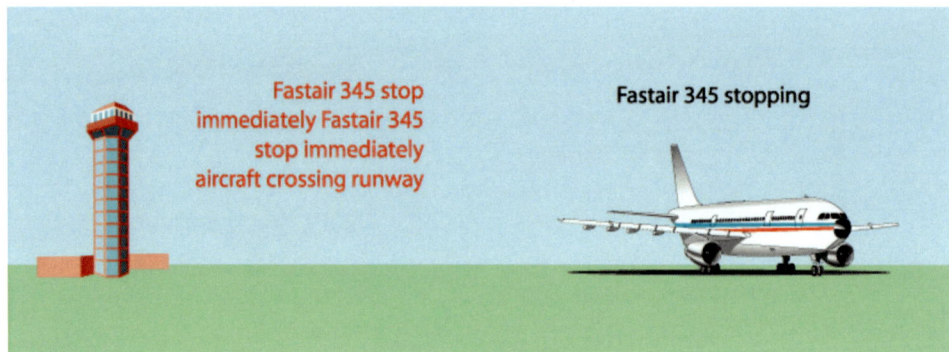

Figure 6.14   Stopping

When a pilot abandons the take-off manoeuvre, the control tower should be so informed as soon as practicable, by use of the word "STOPPING" and assistance or taxi instructions should be requested as required

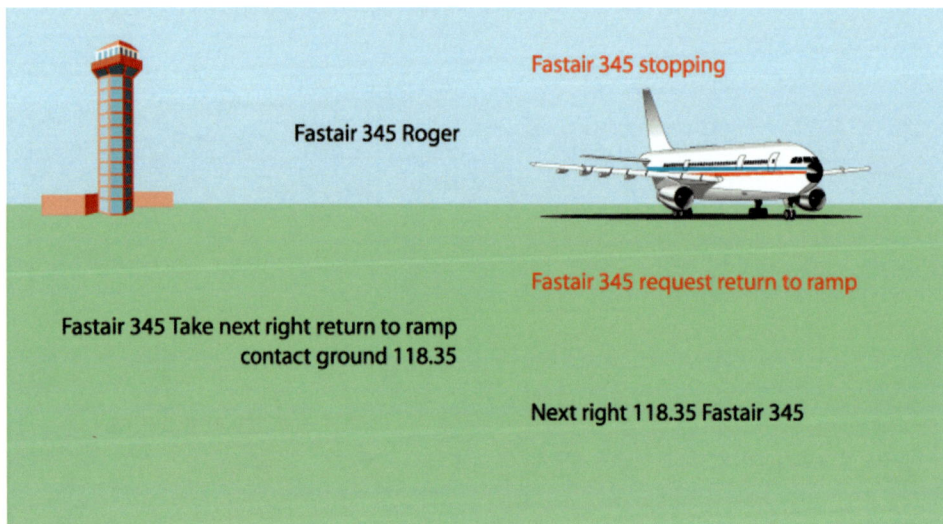

Figure 6.15 Stopping

6.2.4   Aerodrome Traffic Circuit

Requests for circuit joining instructions should be made in sufficient time to allow for a planned entry into the circuit, taking other traffic into account. When the traffic circuit is a right-hand pattern, it should be specified. A left-hand pattern need not be specified, although it may be advisable to do so if there has been a recent change where the circuit direction is variable.

CRANFIELD AVIATION TRAINING SCHOOL LTD. PART-FCL ATO N° 0136
CATS INNOVATION CENTRE, LUTON, Bedfordshire LU2 8DL U.K.   www.catsaviation.com

6-9

Communications

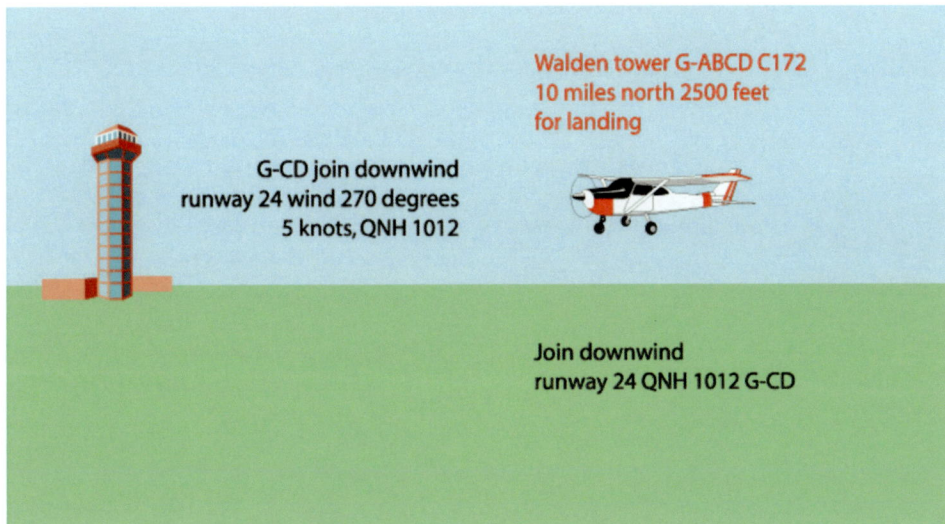

Walden tower G-ABCD C172
10 miles north 2500 feet
for landing

G-CD join downwind
runway 24 wind 270 degrees
5 knots, QNH 1012

Join downwind
runway 24 QNH 1012 G-CD

Figure 6.16   Joining instructions

Where ATIS is provided, receipt of the broadcast should be acknowledged in the initial call to the aerodrome.

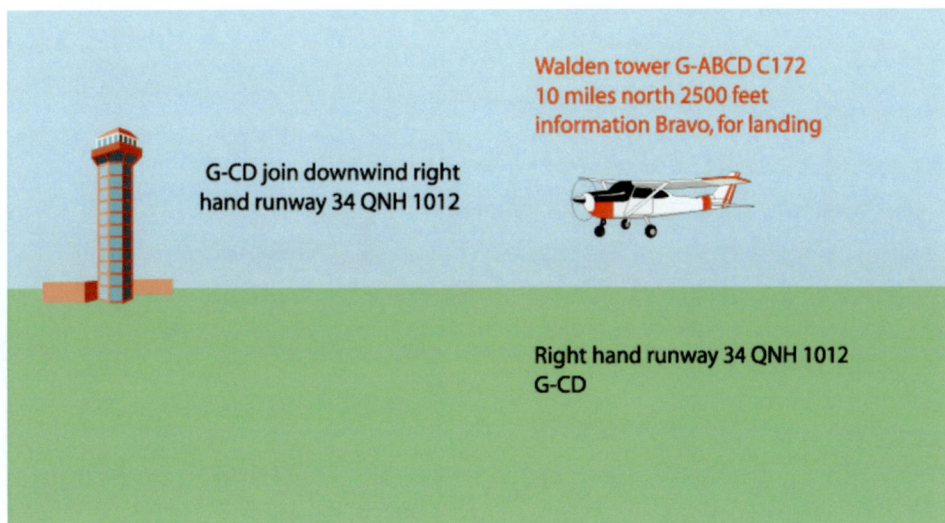

Walden tower G-ABCD C172
10 miles north 2500 feet
information Bravo, for landing

G-CD join downwind right
hand runway 34 QNH 1012

Right hand runway 34 QNH 1012
G-CD

Figure 6.17   Confirming receipt of ATIS

Depending on prevailing traffic conditions and the direction from which an aircraft is arriving, it may be possible to give a straight-in approach.

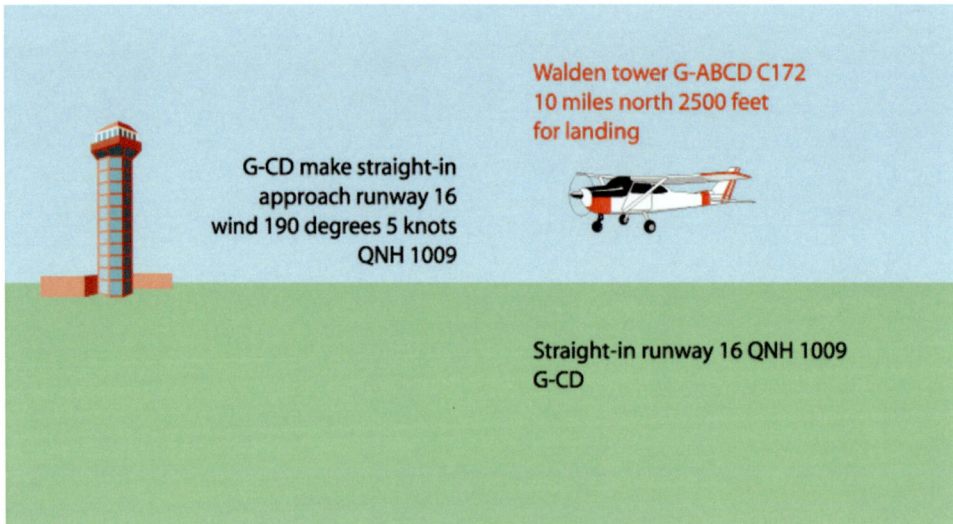

Figure 6.18   Landing clearance

The pilot, having joined the traffic circuit makes routine reports as required by local procedures.

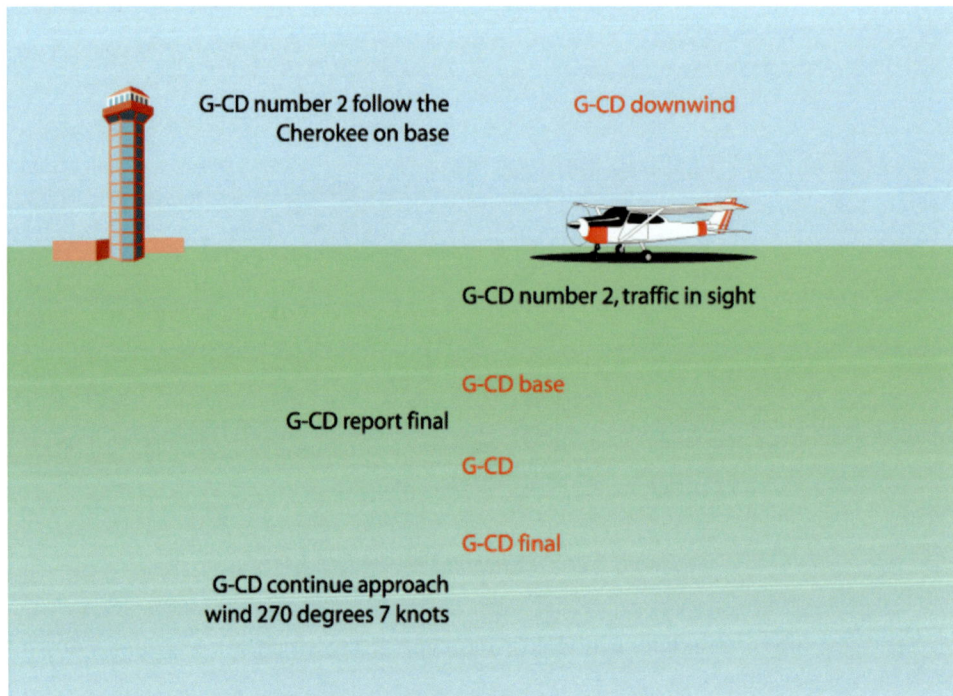

Figure 6.19   Circuit calls

It may be necessary, in order to co-ordinate traffic in the circuit, to issue delaying or expediting instructions.

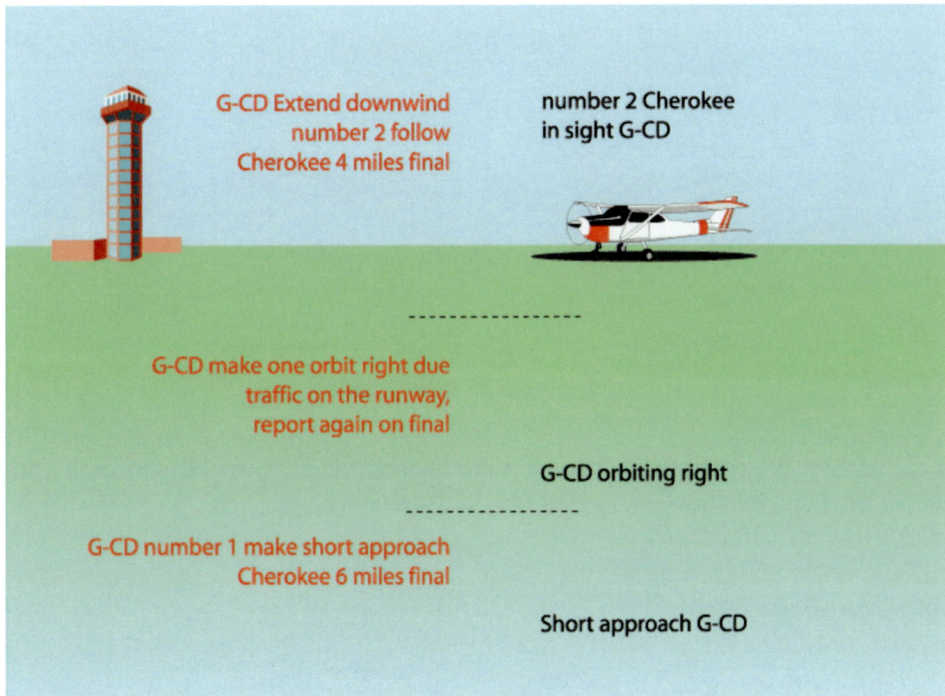

Figure 6.20   Circuit calls

6.2.5 Final Approach and Landing

A "FINAL" report is made when an aircraft turns onto final within 7 KM (4 NM) from touchdown. If and when the turn onto final is made at a greater distance, a "LONG FINAL" report is made; If the aircraft is making a straight-in-approach, a "LONG FINAL" report is made at about 15 KM (8 NM) from touchdown. If no landing clearance is received at that time, a "FINAL" report is made at 7 KM (4 NM) from touchdown.

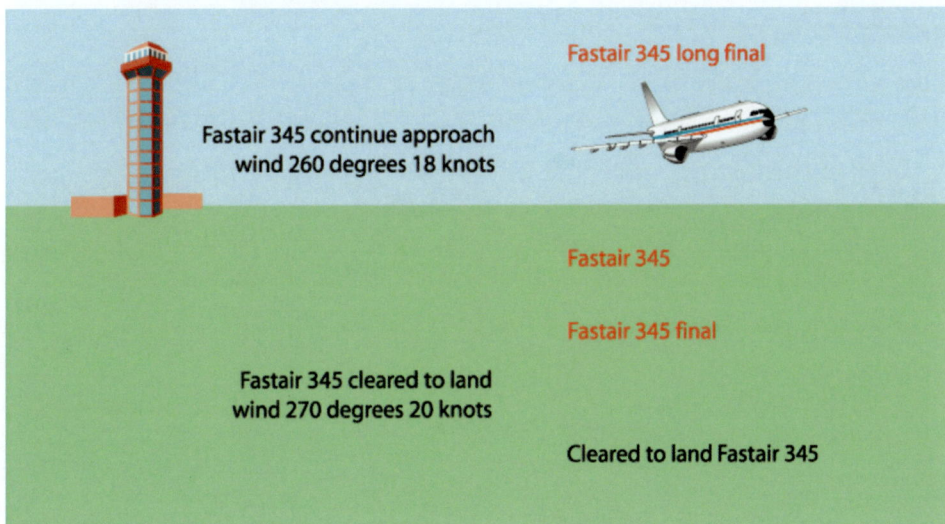

Figure 6.21   Final

A pilot may request to fly past the control tower or other observation point, for the purpose of visual inspection from the ground.

Figure 6.22   Low pass

If the low pass is made for the purpose of observing the undercarriage, one of the following replies could be used to describe its condition but these examples are not exhaustive:

- LANDING GEAR APPEARS DOWN
- RIGHT (or LEFT, or NOSE) WHEEL APPEARS UP (or DOWN)
- WHEELS APPEAR UP (or DOWN)
- RIGHT (or LEFT, or NOSE) WHEEL DOES NOT APPEAR UP (or DOWN)

For training purposes, a pilot may request permission to make an approach along or parallel to the runway, without landing.

Figure 6.23   Low approach

In order to save taxiing time when flying training in the traffic, circuit pilots may request to carry out a "TOUCH AND GO", i.e. the aircraft lands, continues rolling and takes-off, without stopping.

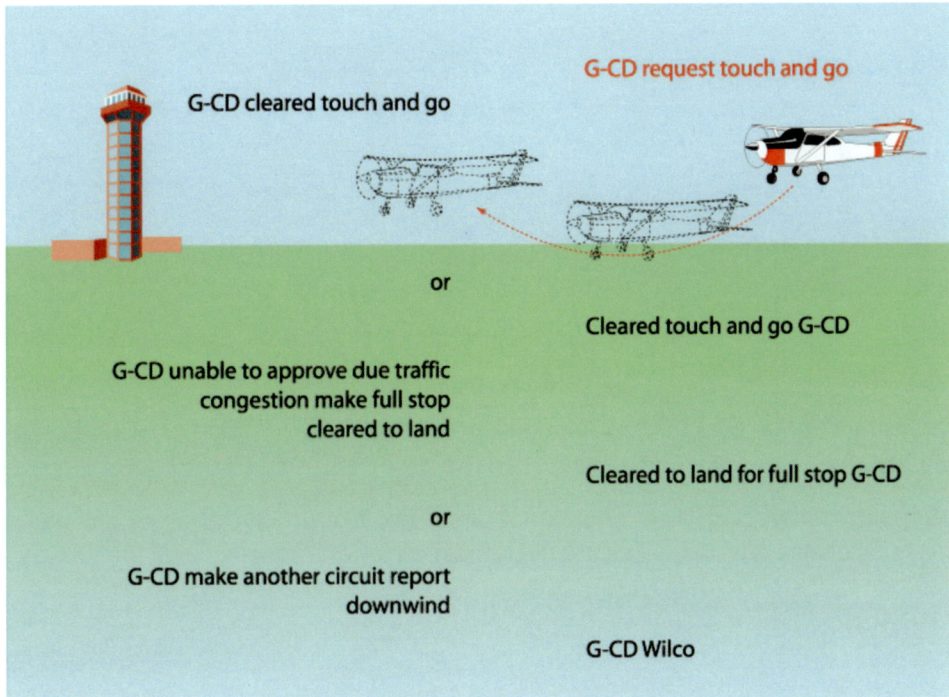

Figure 6.24   Touch and go

6.2.6 Go Around

Instructions to carry out a missed approach may be given to avert an unsafe situation. When a missed approach is initiated cockpit workload is inevitably high. Any transmissions to aircraft going around should be brief and kept to a minimum.

Figure 6.25   Go-around

Unless instructions are issued to the contrary, an aircraft on an instrument approach will carry out the missed approach procedure and an aircraft operating VFR will continue in the normal traffic circuit. In the event that the pilot initiates the missed approach the phrase "GOING AROUND
" shall be used.

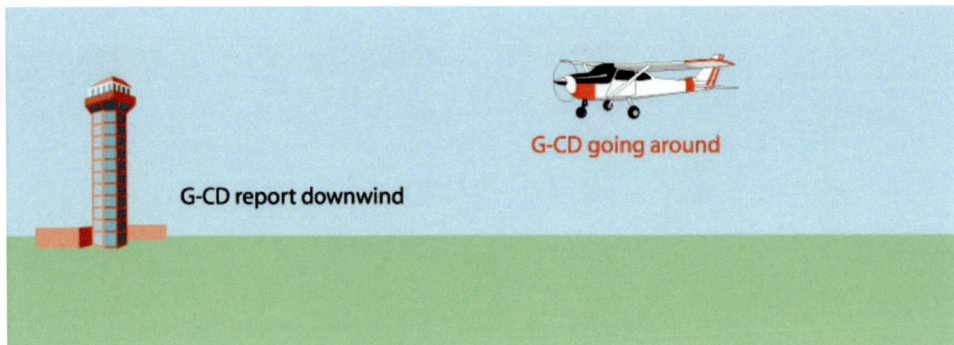

Figure 6.26   Going around

6.2.7   After Landing

Unless absolutely necessary, controllers should not direct taxi instructions to pilots until the landing roll is completed. Unless otherwise advised, pilots should remain on tower frequency until the runway is vacated.

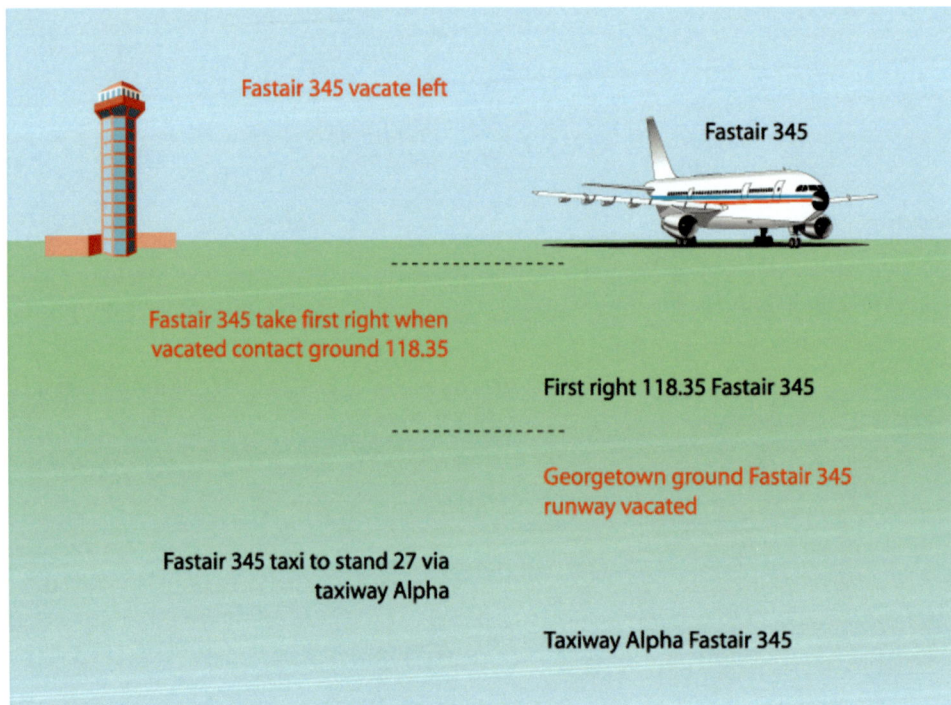

Figure 6.27   After landing

6.2.8   Essential Aerodrome Information

Essential aerodrome information is information regarding the manoeuvring area and its associated facilities which is necessary to ensure the safe operation of aircraft

Essential aerodrome information should be passed to aircraft whenever possible prior to start-up or taxi and prior to the commencement of final approach. It includes information regarding the following:
- construction or maintenance work on, or immediately adjacent to the manoeuvring area;
- rough or broken surfaces on a runway or a taxiway, whether marked or not;
- snow or ice on a runway or a taxiway;
- water on a runway;

- snow banks or drifts adjacent to a runway or a taxiway;
- other temporary hazards, including parked aircraft and birds on the ground or in the air;
- failure or irregular operation of part or all of the aerodrome lighting systems;
- any other pertinent information.

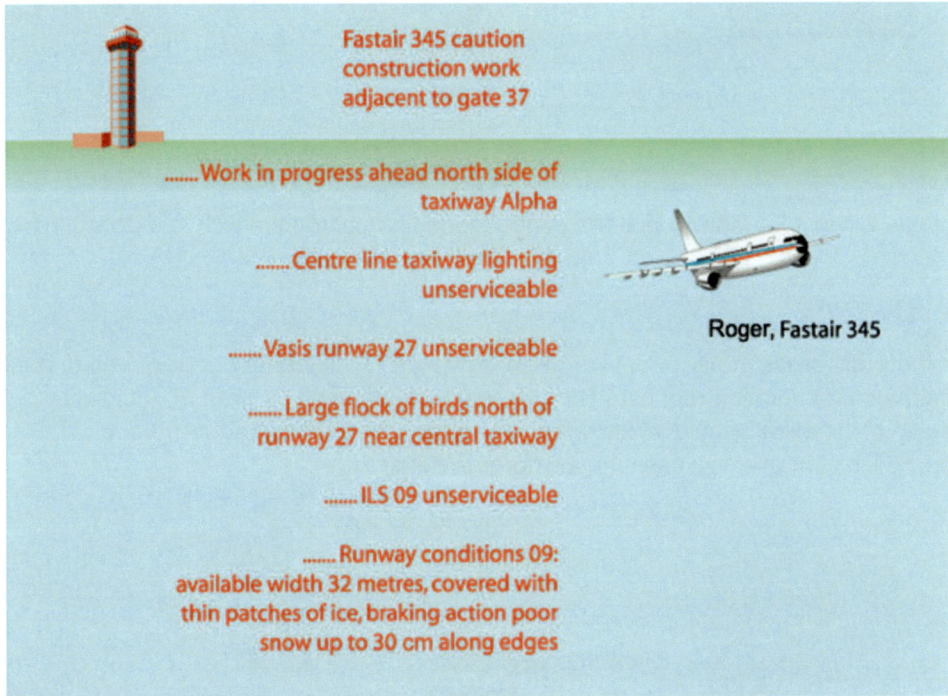

Figure 6.28   Essential aerodrome information

6.3   VFR Departures

Departing VFR flights, when handled by approach control, may be passed information on relevant known traffic in order to assist the pilots in maintaining their own separation.

Pilots should report leaving the area of jurisdiction of the approach control unit.

Figure 6.29   Leaving the control zone

G-CD leave control zone special VFR via route Whiskey, 3000 feet or below, report Whiskey one

Special VFR, route Whiskey 3000 feet or below, will report Whiskey one G-CD

G-CD

Figure 6.30   Special VFR

Special VFR flights will be cleared to leave the control zone, in accordance with laid down procedures.

6.4   VFR Arrivals

Depending on the procedures in use, the pilot of an arriving VFR flight may be required to establish contact with the approach control unit and request instructions before entering its area of jurisdiction. Where there is an ATIS broadcast, the pilot should acknowledge if it has been received; where no ATIS broadcast is provided the approach controller will pass the aerodrome data.

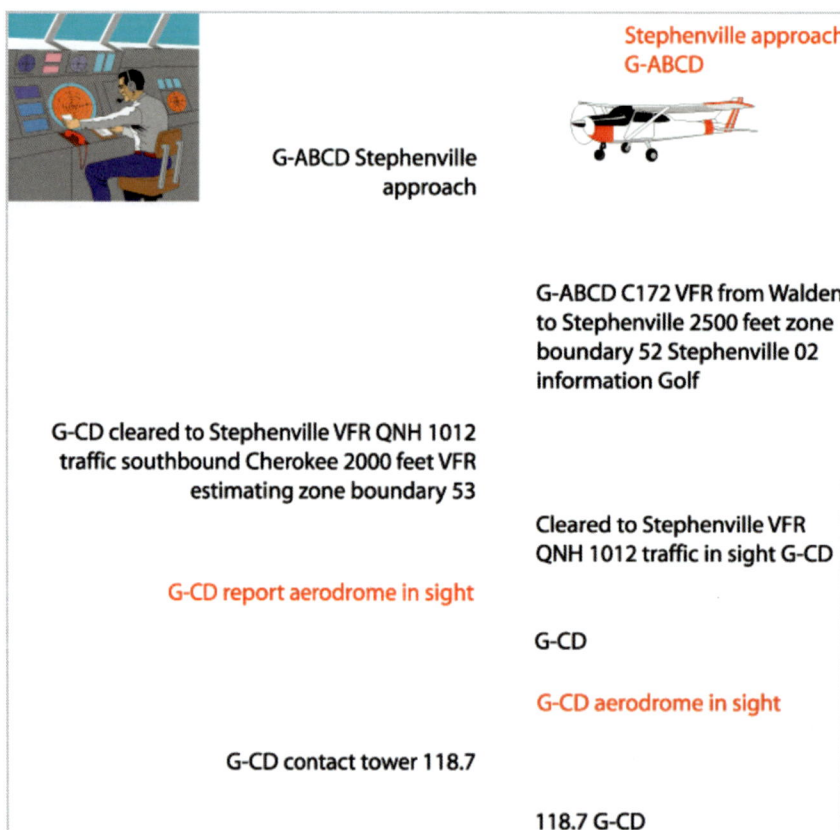

Stephenville approach G-ABCD

G-ABCD Stephenville approach

G-ABCD C172 VFR from Walden to Stephenville 2500 feet zone boundary 52 Stephenville 02 information Golf

G-CD cleared to Stephenville VFR QNH 1012 traffic southbound Cherokee 2000 feet VFR estimating zone boundary 53

Cleared to Stephenville VFR QNH 1012 traffic in sight G-CD

G-CD report aerodrome in sight

G-CD

G-CD aerodrome in sight

G-CD contact tower 118.7

118.7 G-CD

Figure 6.31   VFR arrivals

6.5   Call Signs

6.5.1   Call Signs for Aeronautical (Ground) Stations

Aeronautical stations are identified by the name of the location followed by a suffix. The suffix indicates the

type of unit or service provided

Unit of service	Call sign suffix
Area control centre	CONTROL
Radar (in general)	RADAR
Approach control	APPROACH
Approach control radar arrivals	ARRIVAL
Approach control radar departures	DEPARTURE
Aerodrome control	TOWER
Surface movement control	GROUND
Clearance delivery	DELIVERY
Precision approach radar	PRECISION
Direction finding station	HOMER
Flight information service	INFORMATION
Apron control / management service	APRON
Company dispatch	DISPATCH
Aeronautical station	RADIO

When satisfactory communication has been established and provided that it will not be confusing, the name of the location or the call sign suffix may be omitted.

6.5.2 Aircraft call signs

An aircraft call sign shall be one of the three following types:

Type	Example
The Characters corresponding to the registration marking of the aircraft	G-ABCD or Cessna G-ABCD
The telephony designator of the aircraft operating agency followed by the last four characters of the registration marking	FASTAIR ABCD
The telephony designator of the aircraft operating agency, followed by the flight identification	FASTAIR 345

After satisfactory communication has been established, and provided that no confusion is likely to occur, aircraft call signs may be abbreviated as follows:

Type	Example
The first and at least the last two characters of the aircraft registration	G-CD or Cessna G-CD
The telephony designator of the aircraft operating agency followed by at least two characters of the aircraft registration	FASTAIR CD
The telephony designator of the aircraft operating agency, followed by the flight identification	No abbreviation FASTAIR 345

An aircraft shall use its abbreviated call sign only after it has been addressed in this manner by the aeronautical station

6.6   Establishment and Continuation of Communications

When establishing communications, an aircraft should use the full call sign of both the aircraft and the aeronautical station.

Figure 6.32   First contact

When a ground station wishes to broadcast information, the message should be prefaced by the call "ALL STATIONS".

Also when an aircraft wishes to broadcast information to aircraft in its vicinity, the message should be prefaced by the call "ALL STATIONS".

No reply is expected to such general calls unless individual stations are subsequently called upon to acknowledge receipt.

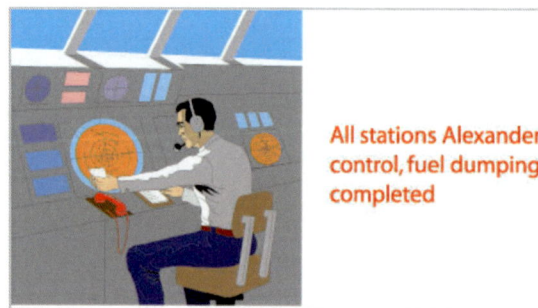

Figure 6.33   All stations call

If there is doubt that a message has been correctly received, a repetition of the message shall be requested either in full or in part.

Phrase	Meaning
• SAY AGAIN	Repeat entire message
• SAY AGAIN … (item)	Repeat specific item
• SAY AGAIN ALL BEFORE … (the first word satisfactorily received)	Repeat part of message
• SAY AGAIN ALL AFTER … (last word satisfactorily received)	Repeat part of message
• SAY AGAIN ALL BETWEEN … AND …	
	Repeat part of message

Figure 6.34   Say again

When a station is called but is uncertain of the identification of the calling station, the calling station should be requested to repeat its call sign until identification is established.

When an error is made in a transmission the word "CORRECTION" shall be spoken, the last correct group or phrase repeated and then the correct version transmitted.

Figure 6.35   Correction

If a correction can best be made by repeating the entire message, the operator shall use the phrase "CORRECTION I SAY AGAIN" before transmitting the message a second time.

After contact has been established, continuous communication may be performed without further identification or call sign until termination of the contact, provided that no confusion or ambiguity will result.

When it is considered that reception is likely to be difficult, important elements of the message should be spoken twice.

Figure 6.36   Words twice

6.7   Transfer of Communications

An aircraft shall be advised by the appropriate aeronautical station to change from one radio frequency to another in accordance with agreed procedures. In the absence of such advice, the aircraft shall notify the aeronautical station before such a change takes place.

Figure 6.37   Tranfser

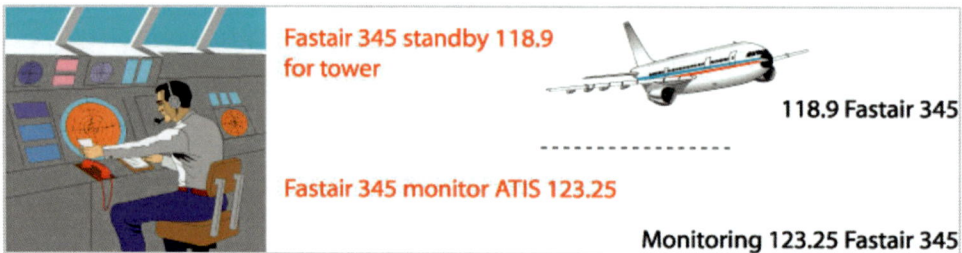

Figure 6.38   Transer

An aircraft may be instructed to "standby" on a frequency when it is intended that the ATS unit will initiate further communications, and to "monitor" a frequency on which information is being broadcast.

6.7.1   Phraseology for transfer of control:

ATC	PILOT
• CONTACT (unit call sign) (frequency)	Pilot repeats
• AT (or OVER) (time or place) CONTACT (unit call sign) (frequency)	Pilot repeats
• IF NO CONTACT (instructions)	Pilot repeats
• STAND BY (frequency) FOR (unit call sign)	Pilot repeats
• WHEN READY CONTACT (unit call sign) (frequency)	Pilot repeats
FREQUENCY CHANGE APPROVED	• REQUEST CHANGE TO (frequency)
• REMAIN THIS FREQUENCY	Pilot repeats
• MONITOR (unit call sign) (frequency)	Pilot repeats

• *Denotes station initiating transmission.*

6.8   Test Procedures

Test transmissions should take the following form:
- The identification of the aeronautical station being called;
- The aircraft call sign;
- The words "RADIO CHECK";
- The frequency being used

Replies to test transmissions should be as follows:
- The identification of the station calling;
- The identification of the station replying;
- Information regarding the readability of the transmission

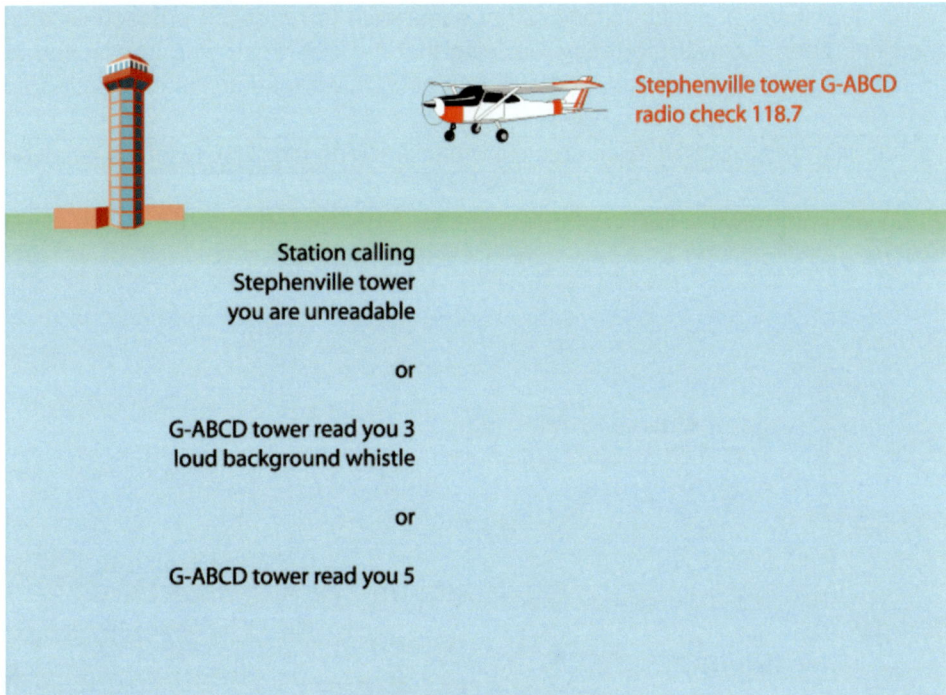

Figure 6.39   Radio check

The readability of transmissions should be classified in accordance with the following readability scale:

1. Unreadable
2. Readable now and then
3. Readable but with difficulty
4. Readable
5. Perfectly readable

When it is necessary for a ground station to make test signals, either for the adjustment of a transmitter before making a call or for the adjustment of a receiver, such signals shall not continue for more than 10 seconds and shall be composed of spoken numbers (ONE, TWO, THREE, etc.) followed by the radio call sign of the station transmitting the test signals. Such transmissions shall be kept to a minimum.

6.9   Issue of Clearance and Readback Requirements

A clearance may vary in content, from a detailed description of the route and levels to be flown, to a brief landing clearance. Controllers will normally pass a clearance slowly and clearly, since the pilot need to write it down and wasteful repetition will thus be avoided. Whenever possible, a route clearance should be passed to an aircraft before start up. In any case, controllers should avoid passing a clearance to a pilot engaged in complicated taxiing manoeuvres and on no occasion should a clearance be passed when the pilot is engaged in line up or take-off manoeuvres. An ATC route clearance is not an instruction to take off or enter an active runway.

The words "TAKE OFF" are used only when an aircraft is cleared for take-off, or when cancelling a take-off clearance. At other times the word "DEPARTURE" or "AIRBORNE" is used

Readback requirements have been introduced in the interests of flight safety. The stringency of the read back requirement is directly related to the possible seriousness of a misunderstanding in the transmission and receipt of ATC clearances and instructions. Strict adherence to readback procedures ensures not only that the clearance has been received correctly, but also that the clearance was transmitted as intended. It also serves as a check that the right aircraft, and only that aircraft, will take action on the clearance.

Clearances to enter, land on, take off from, cross and backtrack on the runway in use, shall be read back

ATC route clearances shall always be read back unless otherwise authorised by the appropriate ATS authority, in which case they shall be acknowledged in a positive manner

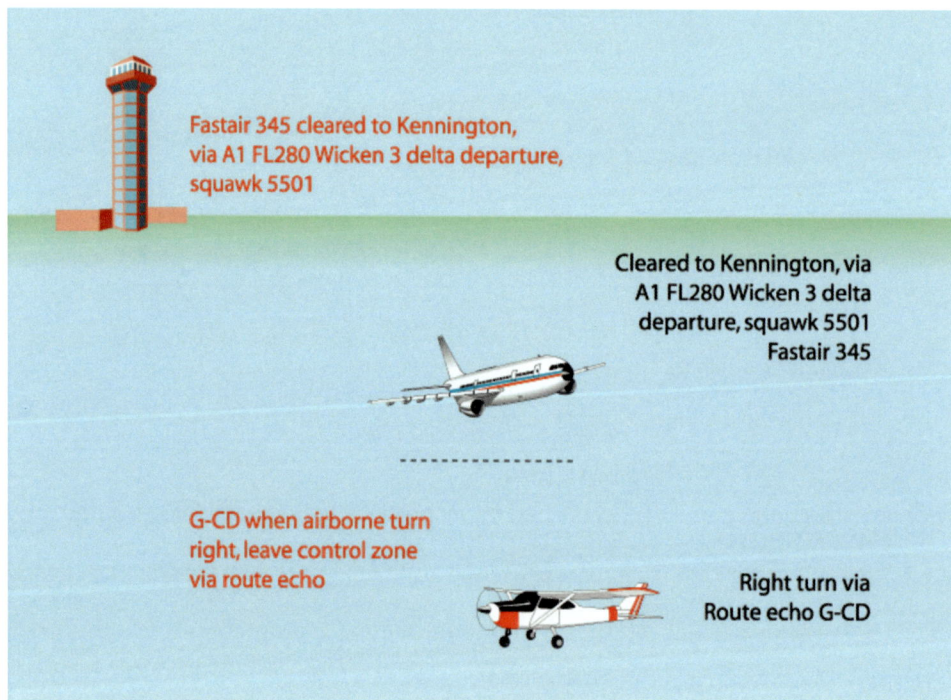

Fastair 345 cleared to Kennington, via A1 FL280 Wicken 3 delta departure, squawk 5501

Cleared to Kennington, via A1 FL280 Wicken 3 delta departure, squawk 5501 Fastair 345

G-CD when airborne turn right, leave control zone via route echo

Right turn via Route echo G-CD

Figure 6.40 Route clearances

The runway in use, heading and speed instructions, level instructions, altimeter settings, SSR codes and where required by ATS authorities, transition levels, shall always be read back

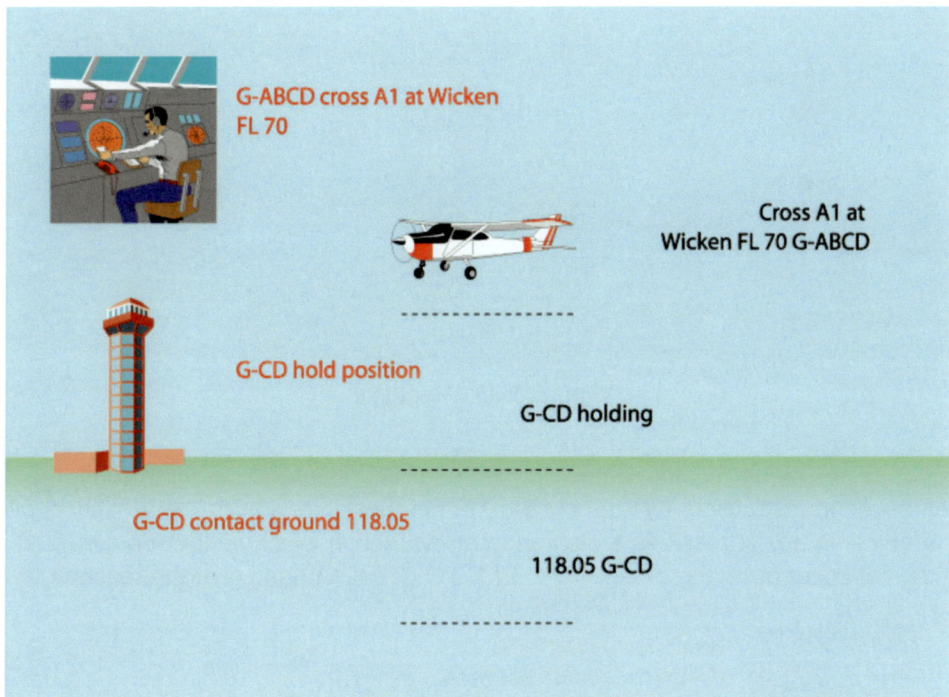

G-ABCD cross A1 at Wicken
FL 70

Cross A1 at
Wicken FL 70 G-ABCD

G-CD hold position

G-CD holding

G-CD contact ground 118.05

118.05 G-CD

Figure 6.41   Readback

Other clearances and instructions (including conditional clearances) shall be read back or acknowledged in a manner that clearly indicates that they have been understood and accepted

An aircraft should terminate the readback with its call sign.

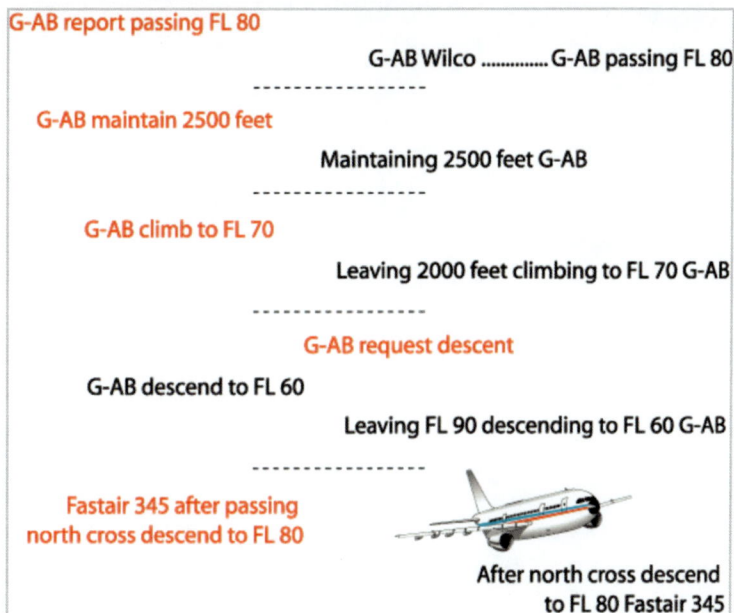

G-AB report passing FL 80

G-AB Wilco .... G-AB passing FL 80

G-AB maintain 2500 feet

Maintaining 2500 feet G-AB

G-AB climb to FL 70

Leaving 2000 feet climbing to FL 70 G-AB

G-AB request descent

G-AB descend to FL 60

Leaving FL 90 descending to FL 60 G-AB

Fastair 345 after passing north cross descend to FL 80

After north cross descend to FL 80 Fastair 345

Figure 6.42   Readback

If an aircraft readback of a clearance or instruction is incorrect, the controller shall transmit the word "NEGATIVE" followed by the correct version.

CRANFIELD AVIATION TRAINING SCHOOL LTD. PART-FCL ATO N° 0136
CATS INNOVATION CENTRE, LUTON, Bedfordshire LU2 8DL U.K.

www.catsaviation.com

CATS

6-24

Communications

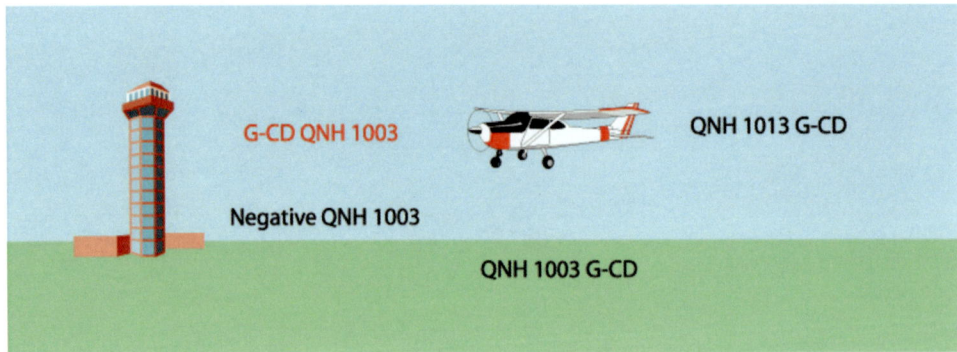

Figure 6.43   Negative

If there is a doubt as to whether a pilot can comply with an ATC clearance or instruction, the controller may follow the clearance or instruction by the phrase "if not possible advise", and subsequently offer an alternative. If at any time a pilot receives a clearance or instruction which cannot be complied with, the pilot should advise the controller using the phrase "UNABLE TO COMPLY" and give the reasons.

Figure 6.44   Unable to comply

CRANFIELD AVIATION TRAINING SCHOOL LTD. PART-FCL ATO N° 0136
CATS INNOVATION CENTRE, LUTON, Bedfordshire LU2 8DL U.K.
6-25

www.catsaviation.com
Communications

CHAPTER 7
General Radar Phraseology

7.1 Introduction

This section contains general radar phraseology that is commonly used in communications between aircraft and all types of radar units. Phraseology that is more applicable to approach radar control or area radar control is described later. The phrase "UNDER RADAR CONTROL" shall only be used when a radar control service is being provided. Normally, however, the call sign suffix used by the radar unit is sufficient to indicate its function. In a radar environment, heading information given by the pilot and heading instructions given by controllers are in degrees magnetic.

7.2 Radar Identification and Vectoring

Radar vectors may be given to establish the identification of an aircraft. Other means of radar identification are the use of position report information, requesting the aircraft to make turns, the use of bearing and distance information from a prominent object or radio aid, and the use of SSR. The pilot should be advised if identification is lost, or about to be lost, and appropriate instructions given.

7.3 Traffic Information and Avoiding Action

Whenever practicable, information regarding traffic on a conflicting path should be given in the following form:
- relative bearing of the conflicting traffic in terms of the 12 h clock code
- distance from the conflicting traffic
- direction of flight of the conflicting traffic
- level and type of aircraft or, if unknown, relative speed of the conflicting traffic, e.g. slow or fast.

Relative movement should be described by using the following terms as applicable: *"closing, converging, parallel, same direction, opposite direction, diverging, overtaking, crossing left to right, crossing right to left."*

Depending on the circumstances, vectors may be offered by the controller or requested by the pilot. The controller should inform the pilot when the conflict no longer exists.

Avoiding action to be taken by the pilot is given when the controller considers that an imminent risk of collision will exist if action is not taken immediately.

7.4 Secondary Surveillance Radar (SSR)

The following phrases and their meanings are instructions that may be given by controllers to pilots regarding the operation of SSR transponders.

Phrase:	Meaning:
SQUAWK (code)	Set the mode A code as instructed
CONFIRM SQUAWK	Confirm mode A code set on the transponder
RECYCLE (code)	Reselect assigned mode A code
SQUAWK IDENT	Operate the "IDENT" feature
SQUAWK MAYDAY	Select the emergency code

SQUAWK STANDBY	Select the standby feature
SQUAWK CHARLIE	Select pressure altitude transmission
CHECK ALTIMETER SETTING AND CONFIRM LEVEL	Check pressure setting and confirm present level
STOP SQUAWK CHARLIE WRONG INDICATION	Deselect pressure altitude transmission feature because of faulty operation
CHECK ID SQUAWK	For a mode S equipped aircraft, check the setting of the aircraft identification feature
VERIFY LEVEL	Check and confirm your level

The pilot's reply to SSR instructions is usually either an acknowledgement or readback. Pilots not in direct communication with ATC should set the applicable special purpose code, preferably before any emergency transmission is made, if the aircraft is equipped with an SSR transponder.

7500 – Hijack or other act of violence
7600 – Radio failure
7700 – Emergency

The AIP of individual countries will contain information of other special purpose SSR codes, if they exist.

7.5 Radar Vectoring

Aircraft may be given specific vectors to fly, in order to establish lateral separation. Unless it is self-evident, pilots should be informed of the reasons why radar vectors are necessary. It may be necessary for ATC purposes to know the heading of an aircraft, as lateral separation can often be established by instructing an aircraft to continue on its existing heading. Conflicting traffic can then be separated laterally. When vectoring is completed, pilots shall be instructed to resume their own navigation and given position information and appropriate instruction as necessary. Occasionally an aircraft may be instructed to make a complete turn (known as an orbit or a 360° turn), for delaying purposes or to achieve a required spacing behind preceding traffic.

7.6 Radar Vectors to Final Approach

Radar vectors are given to arriving flights to position them onto a pilot-interpreted final approach aid, or to a point from which a radar-assisted approach can be made, or to a point from which a visual approach can be made. The approach speed of the aircraft is reduced, in order to ensure adequate separation from the preceding aircraft. Speed adjustment can often reduce the need for radar vectoring, in establishing an approach sequence. Where speed adjustments would be insufficient to ensure correct spacing, it may be necessary to issue additional vectors.

7.7 Surveillance Radar Approach

On a surveillance radar approach (SRA) the pilot is given distances from touchdown, advisory altitude or height information and azimuth instructions, so as to be able to carry out an approach.

Note 1 - Where an SRA procedure terminates at 2 NM from touchdown, the distance from touchdown and advisory altitude checks are normally passed at 1 NM intervals. Where the SRA terminates at less than 2 NM from touchdown, such checks are given each 0.5 NM.

Note 2 - Aircraft replies are expected to all transmissions. However, when the SRA terminates at less than 2 NM from touchdown, the controller's transmissions should not be interrupted for intervals of more than 5 s and aircraft replies are not expected once the aircraft is within 4 NM from touchdown.

Note 3 - When the pilot reports, runway in sight during an SRA and there is reasonable assurance that a landing will be effected, the SRA may be terminated.

7.8 Precision Radar Approach

In a precision radar approach, the controller, in addition to providing heading instructions during the continuous talk-down, provides information on altitude relative to the glide slope, together with instructions on corrective action in the event that the aircraft is too high or too low.

When the radar returns on the elevation element of the PAR indicate that the pilot may be making a missed approach, the radar controller shall, when there is sufficient time to obtain a reply from the pilot, pass the aircraft's height above the glide path and ask the pilot if a missed approach is intended. In similar circumstances, but when there is not sufficient time to obtain a reply from the pilot, the controller should continue the precision approach emphasising the aircraft's displacement. If it becomes apparent that the pilot is making a missed approach, either before or after the normal termination point, the radar controller shall pass missed approach instructions.

CHAPTER 8
Meteorological Information

8.1 Meteorological Information

Meteorological information in the form of reports, forecasts or warnings is made available to pilots using the aeronautical mobile service either by broadcast or by means of specific transmissions from ground personnel to pilots. Standard meteorological abbreviations and terms should be used and the information should be transmitted slowly and enunciated clearly, in order that the recipient may record such data as necessary.

8.1.1 Automatic Terminal Information Service (ATIS)

To alleviate RT loading at busy airports, ATIS messages are broadcast to pass routine arrival and departure information on a dedicated RT frequency or on an appropriate VOR frequency. Pilots inbound to these airports are normally required on first contact with the aerodrome Air Traffic Controller to acknowledge receipt of current information by quoting the code letter of the broadcast. The weather information contained in the ATIS is usually updated every 30 min following the routine weather observations taken at 20 min past the hour and at many airports also at 50 min past the hour.

The ATIS for arriving and departing aircraft will include the following:
- Aerodrome name
- ATIS identification letter
- Time of weather observation
- Type of approach to be expected and runway(s) in use
- Significant runway surface conditions and braking action if appropriate
- Holding delay, if appropriate
- Transition level, if applicable
- Other essential operational information
- Surface wind direction and speed (in magnetic degrees and KT)
- Visibility, and RVR if applicable (in kilometres or metres)
- Present weather (e.g. precipitation)
- Cloud amount below 5000' and height of base (in feet AAL) or CAVOK
- Air and dewpoint temperature (in degrees Celsius)
- Altimeter setting(s)
- Any available information on significant meteorological phenomena in the approach or climb-out areas
- Trend type forecast when available (e.g. NOSIG, TEMPO etc.)
- Specific ATIS instructions

The term CAVOK is used in place of visibility, weather and cloud provided:
- Visibility is 10 KM or more
- There is no cloud below 5000' AAL or below the highest minimum sector altitude, whichever is greater, and no Cumulonimbus clouds
- No precipitation, thunderstorm, shallow fog, or low drifting snow

8.1.2 VOLMET

Meteorological aerodrome reports for certain groups of major aerodromes in the same vicinity that are broadcast on specified VHF or HF frequencies. VOLMET is generally used by aircraft enroute. The information broadcast is the same as in the latest available METAR for the specified stations.

CHAPTER 9
VFR Communication Failure

9.1   Aircraft Communications Failure

When an aircraft station fails to establish contact with the aeronautical station on the designated frequency, it shall attempt to establish contact on another frequency appropriate to the route. If this attempt fails, the aircraft station shall attempt to establish communication with other aircraft or other aeronautical stations on frequencies appropriate to the route or 121.5 MHz (243 MHz on UHF). In addition, an aircraft operating within a network shall monitor the appropriate VHF frequency for calls from nearby aircraft.

If the attempts specified above fail, the aircraft station shall transmit its message twice on the designated frequency(s), preceded by the phrase 'TRANSMITTING BLIND' and if necessary, include the addressee(s) for which the message is intended

In network operation, a message that is transmitted blind should be transmitted twice on both primary and secondary frequencies. Before changing frequency, the aircraft station should announce the frequency to which it is changing.

9.1.1   Receiver failure

When an aircraft station is unable to establish communication due to receiver failure, it shall transmit reports at the scheduled times, or positions, on the frequency in use, preceded by the phrase "TRANSMITTING BLIND DUE TO RECEIVER FAILURE"

The aircraft station shall transmit the intended message, following this by a complete repetition. During this procedure, the aircraft shall also advise the time of its next intended transmission.

9.1.2   Intentions

An aircraft which is provided with air traffic control or advisory service shall, in addition to complying with the procedure above, transmit information regarding the intention of the pilot-in-command with respect to the continuation of the flight of the aircraft.

9.1.3   SSR Selection and Visual Signals

When an aircraft is unable to establish communication due to airborne equipment failure it shall, when so equipped, select the appropriate SSR code (7600) to indicate radio failure. In addition, the aircraft, when forming part of the aerodrome traffic at a controlled aerodrome, shall keep watch for such instructions as may be issued by visual signals.

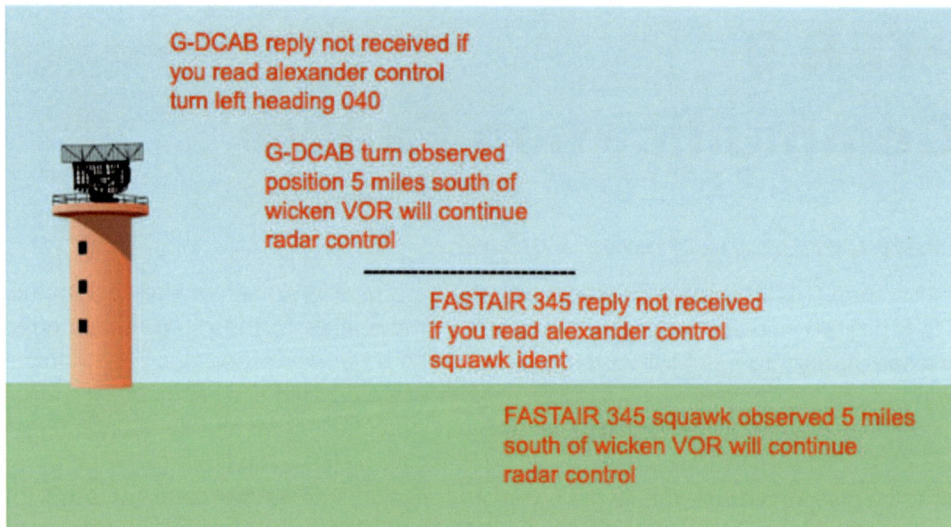

Figure 9.1   Radio failure

CHAPTER 10
Distress and Urgency Procedures

10.1 Introduction

Distress and urgency traffic shall comprise all radiotelephony messages relative to the distress and urgency conditions respectively. Distress and urgency conditions are defined as:

Distress: a condition of being threatened by serious and/or imminent danger and of requiring immediate assistance

Urgency: a condition concerning the safety of an aircraft or other vehicle, or of some person on board or within sight, but which does not require immediate assistance

10.1.1 General Procedures

The radiotelephony distress signal MAYDAY and the radiotelephony urgency signal PAN PAN shall be used at the commencement of the first distress and urgency communication respectively. Distress and urgency traffic shall normally be maintained on the frequency on which such traffic was initiated until it is considered that better assistance can be provided by transferring that traffic to another frequency.

Note: 121.5 MHz or alternative available UHF (e.g. 243 MHz) or HF frequencies may be used as appropriate.

10.1.2 Action by an aircraft in DISTRESS

In addition to being preceded by the radiotelephony distress signal MAYDAY, preferably spoken three times, the distress message to be sent by an aircraft in distress shall be on the air-ground frequency in use at the time and consist of as many as possible of the following elements spoken distinctly and, if possible, in the following order:

- name of the station addressed (time and circumstances permitting);
- the identification of the aircraft;
- the nature of the distress condition;
- intention of the person in command;
- present position, level (i.e. flight level, altitude, etc., as appropriate) and heading

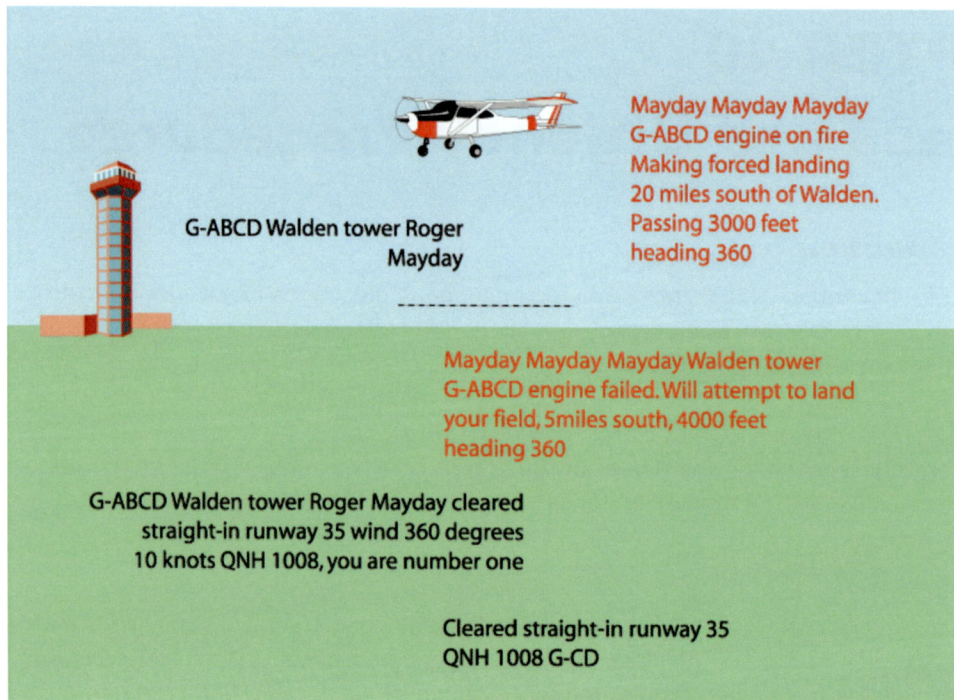

Figure 10.1   MAYDAY MAYDAY MAYDAY

10.1.3 Actions by the first station acknowledging the distress message

The following actions shall be taken by the first station acknowledging a distress message:
- immediately acknowledge the distress message
- take control of the communications or specifically and clearly transfer that responsibility, advising the aircraft if a transfer is made
- take immediate action to ensure that all necessary information is made available, as soon as possible, to:
- the ATS unit concerned
- the aircraft operating agency concerned, or its representative, in accordance with pre-established arrangements
- warn other stations, as appropriate, in order to prevent the transfer of traffic to the frequency of the distress communication.

10.1.4 Imposition of silence

The station in distress, or the station in control of distress traffic, shall be permitted to impose silence, either on all stations of the mobile service in the area or on any station that interferes with the distress traffic. It shall address these instructions "to all stations", or to one station only, according to circumstances. In either case, it shall use:
- STOP TRANSMITTING
- the radiotelephony distress signal MAYDAY

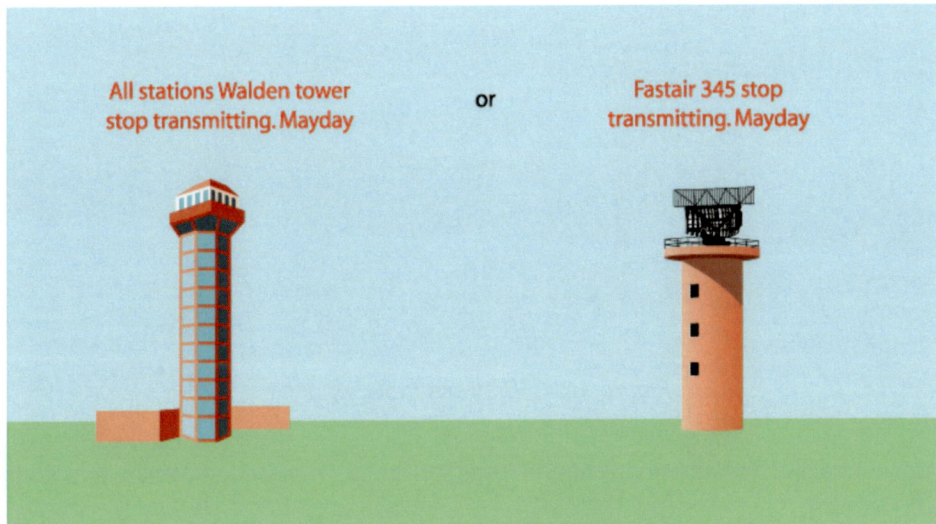

Figure 10.2   Stop transmitting

10.1.5 Action by all other stations

The distress communications have absolute priority over all other communications, and a station aware of them shall not transmit on the frequency concerned, unless:
- the distress is cancelled or the distress traffic is terminated
- all distress traffic has been transferred to other frequencies
- the station controlling communications gives permission
- it has itself to render assistance.

10.1.6 Termination of distress communications and of silence

When an aircraft is no longer in distress, it shall transmit a message cancelling the distress condition.

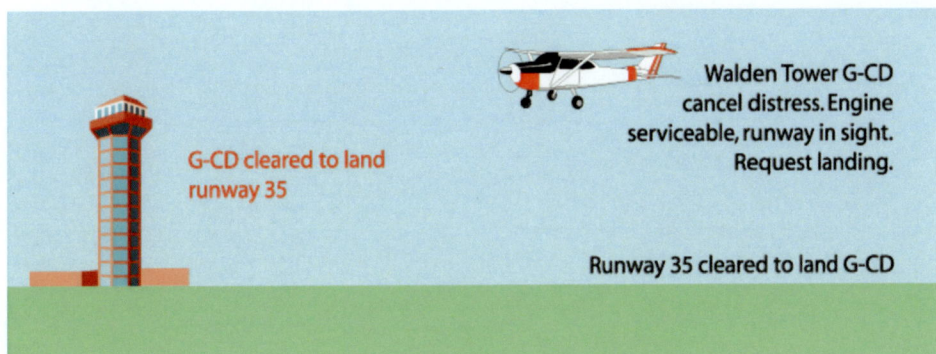

Figure 10.3   Termination of distress

The distress communication and silence conditions shall be terminated by transmitting a message, including the words "DISTRESS TRAFFIC ENDED', on the frequency or frequencies being used for the distress traffic.

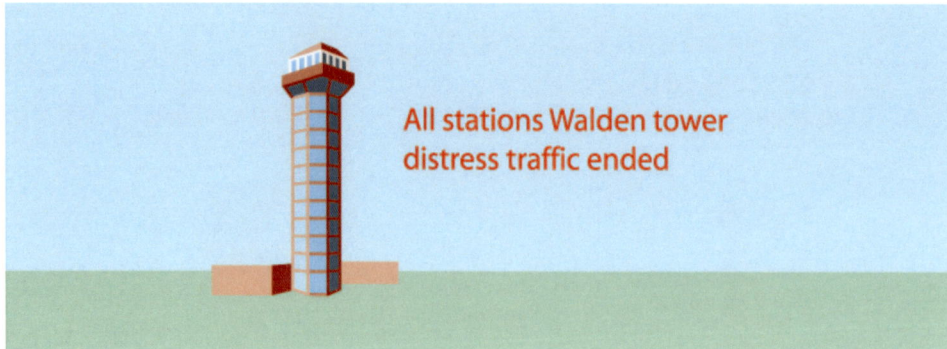

Figure 10.4   Distress traffic ended

Only the station controlling the communications shall originate a message which terminates a distress condition

10.1.7 Action by an aircraft reporting an URGENCY condition

In addition to being preceded by the radiotelephony urgency signal PAN PAN preferably spoken three times, the urgency message to be sent by an aircraft reporting an urgency condition shall be on the air-ground frequency in use at the time and consist of as many as required of the following elements spoken distinctly and, if possible, in the following order:

- the name of the station addressed
- the identification of the aircraft
- the nature of the urgency condition
- the intention of the person in command
- present position, level (i.e. flight level, altitude, etc., as appropriate) and heading
- any other useful information

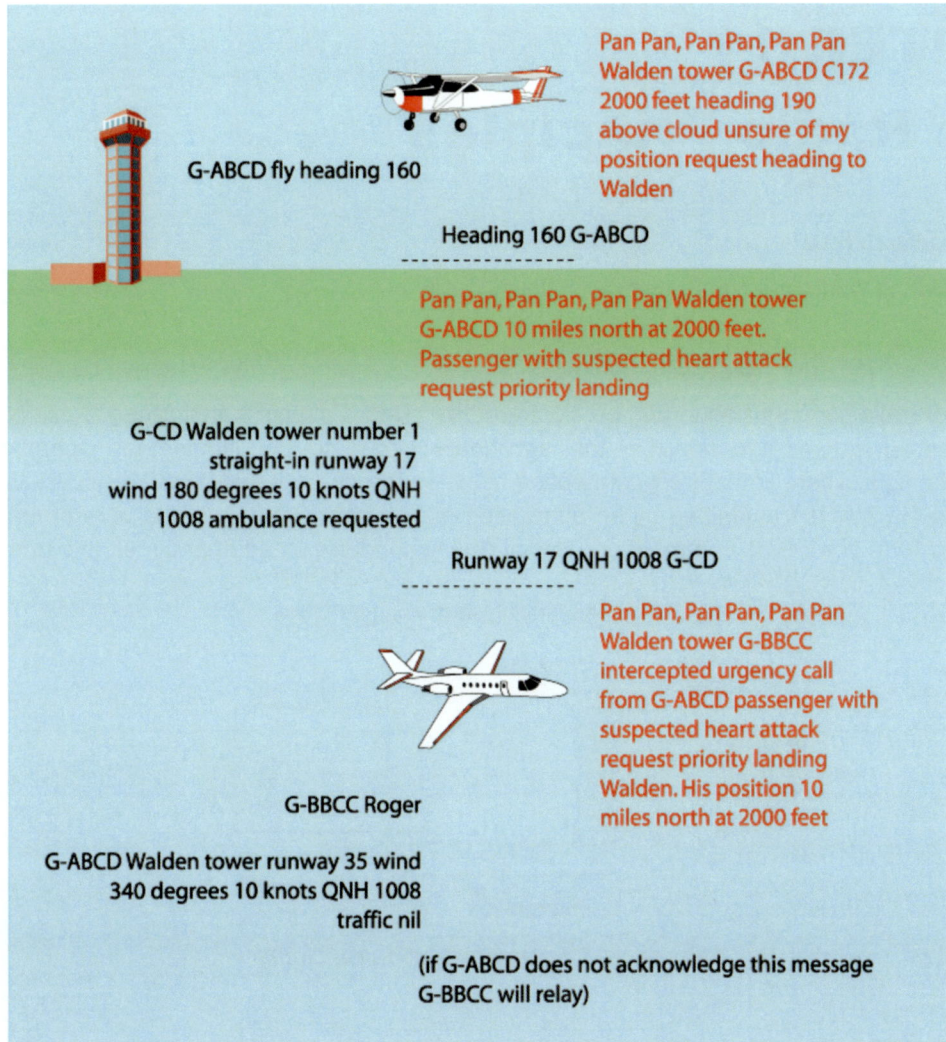

Figure 10.5 PAN PAN, PAN PAN, PAN PAN

10.1.8 Actions by the first station acknowledging the urgency message

The following actions shall be taken by the first station acknowledging an urgency message:
- acknowledge the urgency message
- take immediate action to ensure that all necessary information is made available, as soon as possible, to:
- the ATS unit concerned
- the aircraft operating agency concerned, or its representative, in accordance with pre-established arrangements
- if necessary, exercise control of communications.

The urgency communications have priority over all other communications, except distress, and all stations shall take care not to interfere with the transmission of urgency traffic

CHAPTER 11
Basic Radio Principles

11.1 Introduction

A brief discussion of basic radio fundamentals follows:

11.1.1 Transformer Analogy

The principle of radio communication can be illustrated by using a simple transformer. Closing the switch in the primary circuit causes the lamp in the secondary circuit to be illuminated. Opening the switch extinguishes the light. There is no direct connection between the primary and secondary circuits. The energy that illuminates the light is transmitted by an alternating electromagnetic field in the core of the transformer. This is a simple form of wireless control of one circuit (the secondary) by another circuit (the primary).

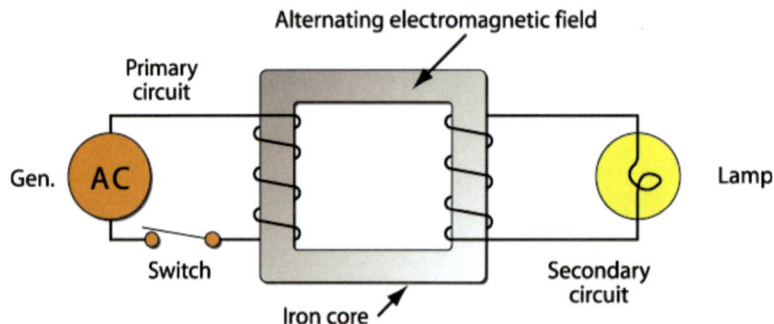

Figure 11.1 A simple transformer circuit

11.1.2 Basic Concept

The basic concept of radio communications involves the transmission and reception of electromagnetic (radio) energy waves through space. Alternating current passing through a conductor creates electromagnetic fields around the conductor. Energy is alternately stored in these fields and returned to the conductor. As the frequency of current alternation increases, less and less of the energy stored in the field returns to the conductor. Instead of returning, the energy is radiated into space in the form of electromagnetic waves. A conductor radiating in this manner is called the transmitting antenna.

11.1.3 Antenna Radiation

For an antenna to radiate efficiently, a transmitter must supply it with an alternating current of the selected frequency. The frequency of the radio wave radiated, will be equal to the frequency of the applied current. Radio waves are radiated in all directions in much the same way that waves travel on the surface of water into which a stone has been thrown. If a radiated electromagnetic field passes through a conductor, some of the energy in the field will set electrons in motion in the conductor. This electron flow constitutes a current that varies with changes in the electromagnetic field. Thus, a variation of the current in a radiating antenna causes a similar varying current in a conductor (receiving antenna) at a distant location. Any intelligence being produced as current in a transmitting antenna will be reproduced as current in a receiving antenna.

11.1.4 Frequency

For many decades, alternating current frequency was expressed in "cycles per second." This seemed the natural term to indicate the complete reversal of the polarity of the voltage and the direction of flow of the current in alternating current circuits. In recent years, however, this term has been replaced with the term Hertz, which is synonymous with "cycles per second". Larger units are formed in the same manner as for other terms of the metric system.

1 kilohertz (kHz) =   1000 hertz (Hz)
1 Megahertz (MHz) = 1 000 000 Hz or 1000 kHz
1 Gigahertz (GHz) = 1 000 000 000 Hz or 1 000 000 kHz or 1000 MHz

11.2 The Radio Wave

The radio wave is made up of an electrical and a magnetic field whose directions are perpendicular to each other. The direction of motion of the radio wave is perpendicular to both the electric and magnetic fields. That is, the direction of motion is perpendicular to the plane formed by the two fields. The propagating radio wave must contain both a magnetic and an electrical field, alternating in a sinusoidal fashion.

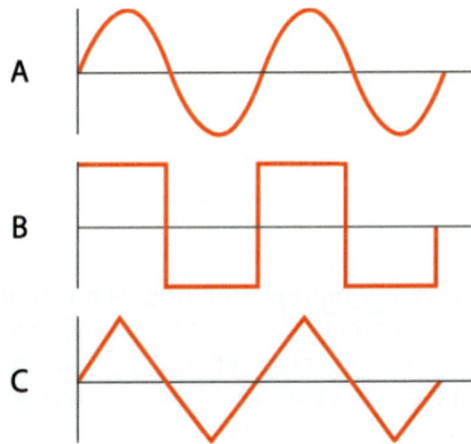

Figure 11.2 Wave Forms

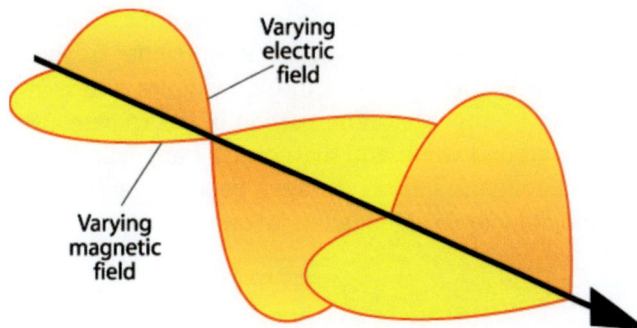

Figure 11.3 Components of a radio wave

11.2.1 Wavelength

The time of completion of one full cycle is equal to the velocity divided by the wavelength. The relationship can be visualised as the greater the wavelength, the lower the frequency. The transmission characteristic of a given electronic system is stated either as wavelength or frequency. The relationship can be expressed as a simple equation:

$$\lambda = \frac{300,000,000}{F}$$

in which λ is the wavelength in metres (m) , F is the frequency in Hertz (Hz), and the constant 300 000 000 (300 x 10^6) is the velocity of light in metres per second.

11.2.2 Propagation and Attenuation

The means by which a radio wave propagates within the Earth's atmosphere varies with its frequency. The wave may be reflected, refracted, diffracted, scattered or absorbed. In the simplest case radio propagation in free space results in a decrease in energy per unit area proportional to the square of the distance between the transmitter and receiver and to the square of the transmitted frequency. The situation, however, is more complicated as the presence of both the ground and of the atmosphere interferes with the free space wave.

11.2.3 Radio Transmission Ranges

Frequencies around 20 kHz can be received at distances of thousands of km. Such transmissions require very large transmitting antennae and their associated narrow bandwidths make them unsuitable for voice communications. At higher frequencies, but below 3 MHz, transmission to moderate distances is primarily along the Earth's surface, this process being more efficient for vertically polarised waves and for those travelling over water. Reflection from the ionosphere enables a useful but variable long-distance facility at frequencies up to about 30 MHz. Frequencies above 100 MHz can transmit signals of greater bandwidth but are limited to line of sight distances. As frequency increases still further absorption effects become significant in the microwave region.

Thus at frequencies above 5 GHz in the presence of rain, snow or fog attenuation is by absorption, depending on the amount of moisture present, the particle size and the transmitted frequency. Above 15 GHz additional attenuation is caused by heavy rain that may limit the path length to only a few km. These higher frequencies are used in radar facilities. At higher frequencies still, selective absorption may occur due to atmospheric water vapour and oxygen, at 23 and 60 GHz respectively.

11.2.4 Ground Waves and Sky Waves

Electromagnetic energy, as transmitted from the antenna, radiates outward in all directions. A portion of this energy proceeds out parallel to the Earth's surface, while the remainder travels upward as well as outward until it strikes one or more layers of ionised gases in the ionosphere and is reflected back to Earth. This normally occurs only once, but may be repeated. The portion of the radiated energy that follows along the surface of the Earth, is called the ground wave and the energy transmitted at higher angles is termed sky waves. In the employment of low frequencies, ground waves become very important, and the conductivity of the Earth's surface becomes a major factor in signal attenuation.

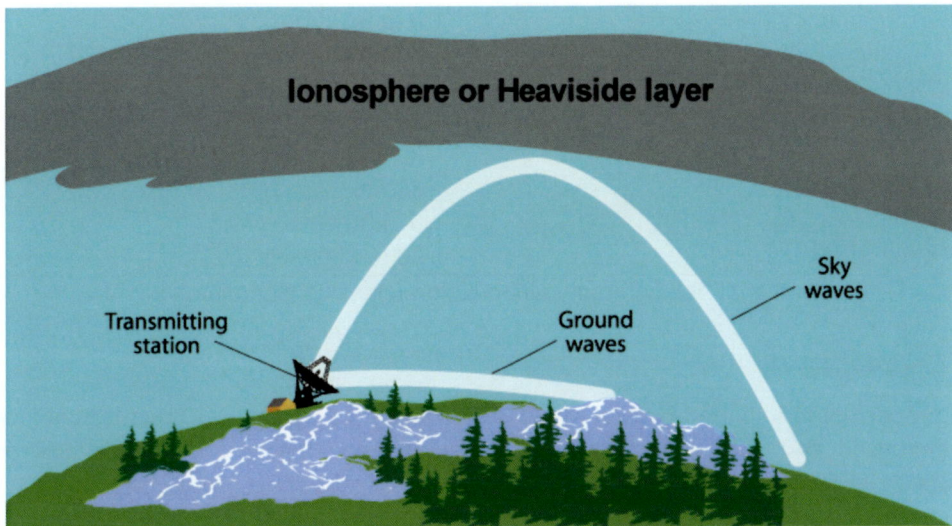

Figure 11.4 Radio wave reflection

11.2.5 Reflection and Refraction

Long-distance transmission of high frequency radio waves, can be achieved by reflection and refraction of the electromagnetic waves from ionised layers in the upper atmosphere. Radio waves and light waves are both forms of electromagnetic waves, differing only in frequency. Almost all surfaces reflect light waves. If the surface is smooth and polished, the light is reflected in a visual fashion, like a mirror. Reflection from a rough surface is diffuse. Dull, dark-coloured surfaces reflect light poorly. When a surface reflects only a portion of the light, the rest is absorbed, and the energy of the absorbed light wave is converted into heat in the material. Radio waves are also reflected, clearly from smooth surfaces and diffusely from rough surfaces. Surfaces of good conductors reflect, and those with poor conductors absorb. The waves pass through some materials that are electrical insulators, such as glass. Most materials do not completely reflect or completely absorb radio waves, but are imperfect reflectors.

In a vacuum in free space, an electromagnetic wave travels in a straight line. When travelling through an area containing matter or material particles, the wave may be bent or refracted. This bending occurs, because the speed of the electromagnetic waves varies slightly, according to the density of the material through which they are moving.

The most important place of refraction of radio waves is in the ionosphere, where particularly, high frequency (HF) band radio waves are susceptible to the process of ionospheric refraction. The amount of refraction of a particular radio signal is not only dependent on its frequency, but also on the state of the ionosphere itself. For any given HF frequency, the strength of the signals returned to the Earth's surface by refraction, can vary from hour to hour and even, minute to minute.

11.3 Frequency Bands

The radio frequency portion of the electromagnetic spectrum extends from approximately 30 kHz to 30 000 MHz. As a matter of convenience, this part of the spectrum is divided into frequency bands. Each band or frequency range produces different effects in transmission.

The Table of 3	
Common Band Name	Frequency Range

VL	Very Low Frequency (VLF)	3 to 30 kHz
L	Low Frequency (LF)	30 to 300 kHz
M	Medium Frequency (MF)	300 to 3000 kHz
H	High Frequency (HF)	3 MHz to 30 MHz
V	Very High Frequency (VHF)	30 to 300 MHz
U	Ultra High Frequency (UHF)	300 to 3000 MHz
S	Super High Frequency (SHF)	3 to 30 GHz
E	Extra High Frequency (EHF)	30 to 300 GHz

Note: The ICAO/ITU (International Telecommunication Union) classification differs slightly.

11.3.1 Low Frequency (LF)

The ionosphere does not reflect the LF band (30 to 300 kHz) very efficiently. Ground losses increase as the frequency is increased and diffraction decreases. Good ground-wave propagation is still possible over moderate distances. LF is utilised by Loran C and NDBs.

11.3.2 Medium Frequency (MF)

The MF band extends from 300 kHz to 3 MHz. Frequencies in this band provide reliable ground-wave propagation over distances up to approximately 700 NM. NDB / locators, make use of the lower end of the MF band.

11.3.3 High Frequency (HF)

The HF band (3 MHz to 30 MHz) is used in long distance communications. This is made possible by reflections from the ionised layers in the ionosphere. Frequencies must be selected, however, with respect to the conditions prevailing at the moment. Under some conditions the higher frequencies travel great distances in the ionosphere, before being refracted sufficiently to reflect the wave back to Earth. The lower frequencies are more suitable at night, while higher frequencies are more suitable at daytime. Aircraft with HF radios should carry publications giving appropriate HF frequencies to use at various times. Expected HF range varies, but can be up to 2000 NM.

11.3.4 Very High Frequency (VHF)

Frequencies in the VHF band (30 to 300 MHz) are used for most aviation communication and aviation navigation. The VHF radio wave has different properties from the ground and sky waves described previously. VHF waves do not "bounce" between the reflecting ionosphere and the Earth's ground. This means that they can only be received by an aircraft on a line of sight position, in relation to the ground stations. The range is limited by the curvature of the Earth and improved by the height of the antenna. VHF offers virtual freedom from atmospheric and precipitation static. The expected or maximum theoretical range (MTR) of the VHF signal can be estimated by this formula:

$$\text{VHF MTR (NM)} = 1.23 \times \left(\sqrt{H_{TX}} + \sqrt{H_{RX}} \right)$$

where H_{TX} = height of transmitter in feet AMSL
 H_{RX} = height of receiver in feet AMSL

or

$$\text{VHF MTR (NM)} = 12 \times \sqrt{Flightlevel}$$

CRANFIELD AVIATION TRAINING SCHOOL LTD. PART-FCL ATO N° 0136
CATS INNOVATION CENTRE, LUTON, Bedfordshire LU2 8DL U.K.   www.catsaviation.com

11-5

Communications

11.3.5 Ultra High Frequencies (UHF)

Frequencies in the UHF band (300 to 3000 MHz) are primarily used for military air / ground voice communications, DME, SSR and ILS glide path transmitters.

11.3.6 Super High Frequency (SHF)

Frequencies in the SHF band (3000 to 30000 MHz) are used for primary radar, radio altimeter, MLS and airport surface movement indicators.

CRANFIELD AVIATION TRAINING SCHOOL LTD. PART-FCL ATO N° 0136
CATS INNOVATION CENTRE, LUTON, Bedfordshire LU2 8DL U.K.

www.catsaviation.com

11-6

Communications

VFR COMMUNICATIONS Self Assessment Test 01

1.   FIR is short for:
A)   Flight Information Region
B)   Flight Information Service
C)   Flight Information Unit
D)   Flight Information Radio

2.   An NDB is a:
A)   Sophisticated DME device
B)   Non-directional radio beacon
C)   Non-directional base line locator
D)   Non-directional back course ILS

3.   VMC is:
A)   Short for Very Marginal Conditions as broadcast by VOLMET
B)   Concerns the way in which instrument flight rules may be interpreted
C)   Short for Visual Meteorological conditions
D)   Only to be used under direct air traffic control

4.   A VASIS indicates through the:
A)   Aircraft ILS system, the attitude and position of the aircraft in relation to the glideslope
B)   Radio Altimeter System, the vertical separation of conflicting air traffic
C)   EICAS the vertical disposition of the aircraft in respect to an airway centre line
D)   Location of lights positioned at the touchdown end of a runway, the vertical disposition of an aircraft with regard to the correct height down the glideslope

5.   The frequency range of a VDF station is:
A)   30 MHz to 300 MHz
B)   10 MHz to 200 MHz
C)   3 MHz to 30 MHz
D)   15 MHz to 400 MHz

6.   VORTAC is:
A)   A combined VOR and TACAN combination where the bearing is from the VOR element and the range from the TACAN element
B)   A combined VOR and TACAN combination where the bearing is from the TACAN and the range from the VOR
C)   Range and bearing are supplied from the TACAN element and the VOR is a switch on device
D)   TACAN refined for missed approach positioning

7.   A Notice to Airmen (NOTAM) is issued when:
A)   A TAF is not available
B)   An actual weather report is unavailable within the next period of 6 hours
C)   Information concerning the establishment, condition or change in any aeronautical facility, service, procedure or hazard needs to be promulgated
D)   A passenger shortfall is evident at the booking in stage

8.   The standard frequency range for UHF communications is:
A)   30 to 300 MHz
B)   10 to 40 MHz
C)   3000 to 6000 MHz
D)   300 to 3000 MHz

9.   A SIGMET is issued when:

A) Snow is forecast at the destination airport
B) Significant weather phenomena which may affect the safety of the aircraft is forecast for en-route operations
C) SST operations are inhibited by significant solar activity
D) Passenger handling is unavailable during the silent hours

10. The standard frequency range for HF communications is:
A) 30 to 300 MHz
B) 300 to 3000 MHz
C) 3 to 30 MHz
D) 3000+ MHz

11. CAVOK means:
A) No cloud below 5000' or below the minimum sector altitude, whichever is greater; no CB, thunderstorms or precipitation; visibility 10 km or more, no shallow fog, or low drifting snow
B) The runway is dry
C) No destination diversion is available
D) No departure airfield diversion is available

12. UTC:
A) concerns the availability of aircraft towing facilities
B) is an abbreviation for co-ordinated universal time
C) concerns the notification of the closure of taxiways
D) concerns the way in which the Earth is divided into time zones and the positioning of the International Date Line

13. ETA is short for:
A) Estimated terminal arrival time
B) Estimated terminal approach time
C) Estimated time of arrival
D) Equivalent time zone actual weather prefix

14. A METAR is:
A) A destination alternate weather forecast
B) A departure point weather forecast
C) An actual en-route weather report
D) An actual airfield meteorological report

15. ATIS is:
A) A secondary surveillance radar device
B) Mode C
C) Automatic Terminal Information Service
D) Provided by VOLMET

16. RCC is:
A) A VOLMET service
B) A Rescue Co-ordination Centre
C) An ATIS Service
D) Concerns radiation warnings and is measured in milli-rems or milli-Sieverts

17. A VOLMET service provides:
A) Meteorological information for aircraft in flight
B) Company operations information prior to departure
C) Company information prior to arrival at destination
D) Advises Flight Crew on the availability of Customs officials at first point of entry into the USA

18. When an aircraft lands with QNH set the altimeter will read:
A) Zero

B)   Flight Level
C)   Airfield elevation
D)   QFE and is the same as QNH

19.   SSR is:
A)   Primary surveillance radar
B)   Secondary surveillance radar
C)   Supersonic operations requirement
D)   To do with METAR and TAF information

20.   A standard instrument arrival is known as a:
A)   SIA
B)   SDP
C)   SA
D)   STAR

VFR COMMUNICATIONS Self Assessment Test 01 ANSWERS

1	A
2	B
3	C
4	D
5	A
6	A
7	C
8	D
9	B
10	C
11	A
12	B
13	C
14	D
15	C
16	B
17	A
18	C
19	B
20	D

CRANFIELD AVIATION TRAINING SCHOOL LTD. PART-FCL ATO N° 0136
CATS INNOVATION CENTRE, LUTON, Bedfordshire LU2 8DL U.K.

www.catsaviation.com

11-10

Communications

VFR COMMUNICATIONS Self Assessment Test 02

1. The production of a radio transmission can be likened to the operation of a switchable:
A) AC electric motor
B) Transformer
C) DC motor
D) DC generator

2. One megahertz (MHz) is equal to:
A) 1000 Hz
B) 10 000 Hz
C) 1 000 000 Hz or 1000 kHz
D) 10 000 000 Hz

3. An aerial is supplied with:
A) DC power
B) AC and DC power
C) AC current
D) An effective halve wave unmodulated carrier wave

4. The radiation fields of an aerial consist of two varying elements that are perpendicular to each other:
A) The magnetic and electrical fields
B) The stator and rotor fields
C) The magnetic and isogonal fields
D) A variable carrier wave with a toroidal transmitter

5. Wavelength can be determined from the formula:
    Note: In some text books, the symbol for the basic radio wave frequency is C. For calculations, use 300×10^6 m s^{-1} and refer all dimensions to metres:
A) $\lambda = C / F$
B) $C / \lambda = \lambda$
C) $C / \lambda = \lambda^2$
D) $F / C = \lambda$

6. Which of the following statements is correct:
A) The higher the frequency of a radio wave the longer the range
B) The higher frequencies do not penetrate the ionosphere
C) The lower the frequency the longer the range and the highest frequencies are attenuated by moisture and are used in radar equipment
D) Smooth surfaces are very poor reflectors of radio waves.

7. The maximum theoretical range of a VHF signal can be derived from the following formula:
A) Height of transmitter/height of receiver = the range in meters
B) $1.23 \times [\sqrt{\text{height if transmitter (ft)}} + \sqrt{\text{height of receiver (ft)}}]$
C) $1.23 \times [\text{height of transmitter (ft)} + \text{height of receiver (ft)}]$
D) $1.23 \times [\text{height of transmitter}^2 + \text{height of receiver}^2]$

8. A detector and a discriminator remove the intelligence from the radio waves of:
A) AM sets only
B) FM sets only
C) Radar sets only
D) AM and FM sets respectively

9. The HF radio frequency range is:

A) 108.0 to 117.95 MHz
B) 121.5 to 243 MHz
C) 2850 to 22 000 kHz
D) 2850 to 22 000 MHz

10. The range of a VHF transmitter (in NM) is:
A) $\sqrt{FL}$ x 1.23
B) $\sqrt{1.5}$ x height of the aircraft in meters or the $\sqrt{FL}$ x 12
C) $\sqrt{FL}$ x 12
D) 1.5 x $\sqrt{}$ of the height of the aircraft in feet or the $\sqrt{FL}$ x 12

11. A radio direction finding station will use the following Q code to pass a true heading (no wind) to an aircraft to head for that station:
A) QUJ
B) QGE
C) QTF
D) QDM

12. If QFE is set, the altimeter will read the height above the:
A) Pressure altitude of the stated reference point
B) QFE reference datum
C) Standard pressure level
D) Transition level

13. A Class A bearing is that which is accurate to:
A) 5°
B) 2°
C) 10°
D) 1°

14. A Class B position is accurate to within:
A) 10 NM (6 km)
B) 15NM (9 km)
C) 20 NM (37 km)
D) 30 NM (48 km)

15. The order of priority when passing flight details is as follows:
A) Aircraft type, callsign, position, heading, altitude, conditions, estimate, request
B) Callsign, aircraft type, heading, altitude, estimate, conditions, request, position
C) Callsign, altitude, estimate, request, position, aircraft type, heading, conditions
D) Callsign, aircraft type, position, heading, altitude, conditions, estimate, request

16. The priority of messages, in descending order, is:
A) Distress, urgency, direction finding messages
B) Direction finding messages, distress, urgency
C) Height, speed, condition
D) Flight regularity messages, meteorological conditions

17. An example of the content of a flight regularity message is as follows:
A) Individual requirements of passenger or crew members
B) Messages concerning the servicing of the aircraft
C) Individual dietary requirements of a passenger or crew member
D) Weather on route

18. A PAN message is defined as follows:

A)   A condition of being threatened by serious and/or imminent danger and of requiring immediate assistance
B)   Medical assistance only is required immediately after the aircraft lands
C)   A condition concerning the safety of an aircraft or other vehicle, or of some person on board or within sight, but does not require immediate assistance
D)   PAN is no longer used in aircraft telecommunications

19.   A request 'WORDS TWICE' means that:
A)   Communication is difficult, please send all groups of words twice
B)   As a request, "communication is difficult, please send every word or group of words twice"
C)   The receiver station is being switched off and this will be transmitted twice
D)   The alternative word, "acknowledge" need no longer be used

20.   BREAK BREAK is used to:
A)   Indicate the separation between parts of a message or messages
B)   Acknowledge a diplomatic meaning to a request
C)   Means that hi-jackers are on board and assistance is required after landing
D)   Used when entering a military combat zone under military radar

VFR COMMUNICATIONS Self Assessment Test 02 ANSWERS

1	B
2	C
3	C
4	A
5	A
6	C
7	B
8	D
9	C
10	C
11	A
12	B
13	B
14	C
15	D
16	A
17	B
18	C
19	B
20	A

VFR COMMUNICATIONS Self Assessment Test 03

1. To expedite communications, the use of phonetic spelling should not be used unless:
A) The message is to do with MAYDAY
B) The message is to do with PAN
C) Unless the message is to do with PAN MEDICAL
D) Transmission conditions are poor and intelligibility of the message is distorted

2. In VHF communications the words:
A) OUT and ROGER are not normally used
B) GO AHEAD and I SAY AGAIN are not normally used
C) OUT and OVER are not normally used
D) STANDBY and VERIFY are not normally used

3. A call to a station followed by the suffix ARRIVAL after its call sign is a transmission to:
A) The tower
B) Approach control radar arrivals
C) Clearance delivery
D) Approach control

4. The words READ BACK mean:
A) Repeat all, or the specified part, of this message back to me exactly as received
B) Repeat all of this message back to me
C) Repeat squawk
D) Repeat cleared altitude

5. An aircraft call sign shall be chosen from one of the following possibilities:
A) The registration letters of the aircraft or, the telephony designator of the operating agency
B) The registration letters of the aircraft or, the telephony designator of the aircraft operating agency followed by the registration letters or, telephony designator of the operating agency followed by the flight identification number
C) The telephony designator of the operating agency and the flight identification number only
D) The registration letters of the aircraft only

6. An aircraft call sign may be abbreviated, once contact has been established and provided that no confusion is likely to occur, to the form of:
A) The telephony designator of the operating agency and all registration letters
B) All of the registration letters only
C) The first and at least the last two characters of the registration letters or, the telephony designator of the operating agency and at least two characters of the aircraft registration
D) The telephony designator of the operating agency and the last two numbers of the flight identification

7. When a ground station wishes to broadcast information the message is prefaced by:
A) ALL CALL SIGNS
B) CALL SIGNS...........
C) AIRCRAFT IN MY VICINITY
D) ALL STATIONS

8. If an ALL STATIONS call is made:
A) No reply is expected unless individual stations are asked to acknowledge receipt
B) No reply is ever to be made
C) Acknowledgement of an ALL STATIONS call is mandatory
D) It must be repeated after an acknowledgement of receipt is made

9. The basic phraseology for transfer of control is:

A)   TRANSFER TO (unit call sign - frequency) OVERHEAD (place or time)
B)   CONTROL CHANGE TO (unit call sign - frequency) OVERHEAD (place or time)
C)   CONTACT (unit call sign – frequency) AT (place or time) IF NO contact (instructions)
D)   CHANGE TO (frequency – unit call sign)

10. A route clearance should be ideally passed to an aircraft:
A)   Just prior to take-off so that the pilot gets the latest information
B)   Prior to start when work loads are low, mistakes are less likely to happen and aircraft manoeuvring is not taking place
C)   During the Take-Off Checks
D)   During taxi

11. The words TAKE OFF are only to be used when:
A)   An aircraft is cleared to line-up only
B)   An aircraft is cleared to start
C)   When clearance delivery authorises its use
D)   An aircraft is cleared for take-off or, when cancelling a take-off clearance. At all other times the words DEPARTURE or AIRBORNE is used. Readback is mandatory

12. A radio test procedure consists of the following items:
A)   The station identification being called, the aircraft call sign, the words RADIO CHECK shall be used and the frequency being used
B)   The station identification and the words RADIO CHECK only
C)   The words RADIO CHECK only
D)   The station identification being used, the aircraft call sign and the words RADIO CHECK

13. The readability of test transmissions is classified as follows:
A)   5 – unreadable to 1 – perfectly readable
B)   5 – perfectly readable to 1 – unreadable
C)   Class A – perfectly readable to Class E – unreadable
D)   Class E – perfectly readable to Class A – unreadable

14. A test call shall not continue for more than:
A)   12 s
B)   8 s
C)   10 s
D)   5 s

15. A distress call content is to be as follows:
A)   MAY DAY (three times if possible) on 121.5 MHz

Name of station addressed (if time permits)
Aircraft identification
The nature of the distress condition
The intention of the person in command
Present position
Level
Heading

B) PAN (three times if possible)
Aircraft
Name of station addressed
The aircraft identification
The nature of the distress condition
Intentions
Level
Heading

C) MAY DAY (three times if possible) on the frequency in use at the time
Name of station addressed (if time permits)
The aircraft identification
The nature of the distress condition
The intention of the person in command
Present position
Level (flight level, altitude, height)
Heading

D) MAY DAY (three times if possible) on 243 MHz
The aircraft identification
He intentions of the person in command
Level
Present position
Heading

16. On receiving a distress call, the receiving station shall:
A) Acknowledge and transfer communications control to the aircraft in distress
B) Acknowledge and transfer control of communications to the operating agency
C) Acknowledge and transfer the distress aircraft to another frequency to avoid air traffic control conflict
D) Acknowledge, take control of communications, make sure all information is made available to ATS, the operating agency and warn other stations

17. An urgency call content is to be as follows:
A) PAN PAN (on the frequency in use)
Name of station addressed

Identification of the aircraft
The nature of the urgency condition
The intention of the person in command

B) PAN PAN
Aircraft identification
The intention of the person in command
Heading
Height
Position

C) MAY DAY (three times – this is mandatory)
Heading
Position
Level
Aircraft identification
The intention of the person in command

D) PAN PAN (on 121.5MHz)
Present position
Heading aircraft identification
The intention of the person in command
The identification of the station being called

18. Radar information relating to conflicting traffic should where possible be given in the following form:
A) Relative bearing in degrees T, speed, height and heading of conflicting traffic
B) Relative bearing in clock terms, distance from, direction of flight of conflicting traffic, and level, type and relative speed (slow or fast). Relative movement should be described as closing, parallel, opposite direction etc.
C) Relative bearing in degrees M, speed, height and heading.
D) Relative bearing in degrees left or right, heading, speed, height

19. Wind velocity is transmitted in:
A) Degrees True and mph
B) Degrees True and KT
C) Degrees magnetic and KT
D) Degrees magnetic and mph

20. If an aircraft radio receiver fails the aircraft should:
A) Transmit using the phrase "TRANSMITTING BLIND DUE TO RECEIVER FAILURE" at the scheduled times, or positions on the frequency in use and state the time of the next transmission. The SSR, if fitted, should be selected to 7600
B) As above but squawk 7700
C) As above but squawk 7500
D) None of the above

VFR COMMUNICATIONS Self Assessment Test 03 ANSWERS

1	D
2	C
3	B
4	A
5	B
6	C
7	D
8	A
9	C
10	B
11	D
12	A
13	B
14	C
15	C
16	D
17	A
18	B
19	C
20	A

Section 2
IFR
Communications

CRANFIELD AVIATION TRAINING SCHOOL LTD. PART-FCL ATO N° 0136
CATS INNOVATION CENTRE, LUTON, Bedfordshire LU2 8DL U.K.

www.catsaviation.com

Communications

CHAPTER 12
General Operating Procedures

12.1 Introduction

This chapter contains additional material which is particularly relevant to the IFR communications learning objectives. In some instances, the information required is identical to that covered in VFR communications and reference should be made to the appropriate chapter in *Section 1 – VFR Communications* as necessary.

12.2 Standard Phraseology

12.2.1 Pushback

At many aerodromes at which large aircraft operate, the aircraft are parked nose-in to the terminal, in order to save parking space. Aircraft have to be pushed backwards by tugs before they can taxi for departure.

Requests for pushback are made to ATC or apron control / management service depending on the local procedures.

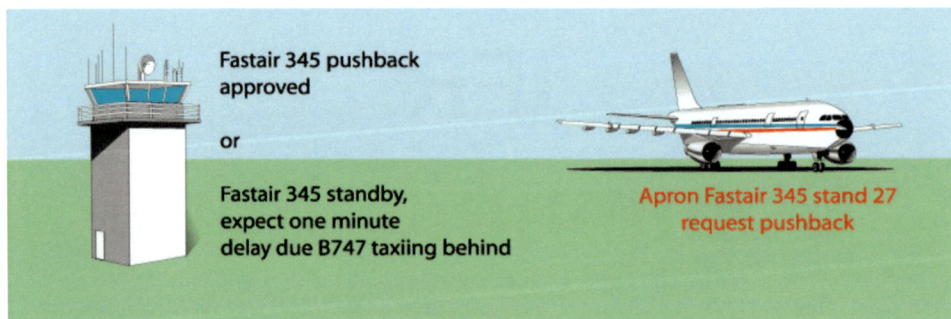

Figure 12.1

The following phraseology should be used by the pilot and the ground crew to co-ordinate the pushback.

CRANFIELD AVIATION TRAINING SCHOOL LTD. PART-FCL ATO N° 0136
CATS INNOVATION CENTRE, LUTON, Bedfordshire LU2 8DL U.K.
12-1

www.catsaviation.com

Communications

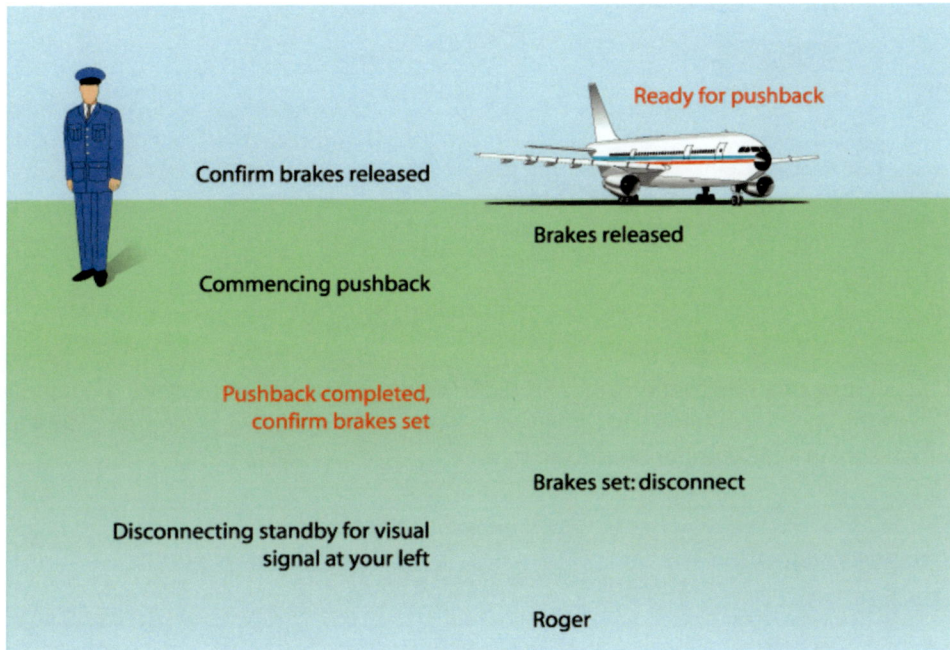

Figure 12.2

When the manoeuvre is complete, the ground crew gives the pilot a visual signal to indicate that the aircraft is free to taxi. Should the pilot wish to stop the manoeuvre at any stage, the phrase "stop pushback" should be used.

12.2.2 Flight Plans

A pilot may file a flight plan with an ATS unit during flight, although the use of busy air traffic control channels for this purpose should be avoided. Details should be passed using the following format:
1. Aircraft identification and type
2. Position and heading
3. Level and flight conditions
4. Departure aerodrome
5. Estimated time at entry point
6. Route and first point of intended landing
7. True airspeed
8. Desired level on airway or advisory route

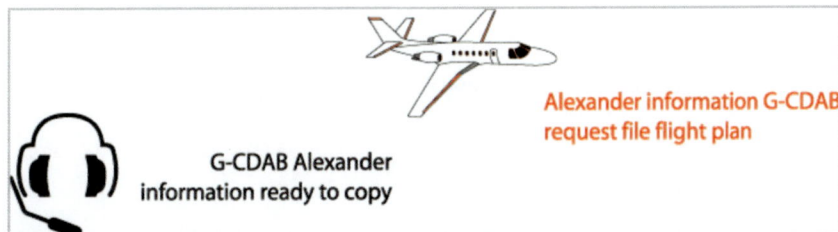

Figure 12.3   Requesting airborne flight plan

G-AB IFR flight plan
cancelled at 47, contact
Alexander information
125.75

Alexander control G-AB
cancelling IFR flight plan.
Proceeding VFR estimating
Stephenville at 1732

Figure 12.4   Cancelling flight plan

During a flight a pilot may change from IFR to VFR flight. When a pilot has expressed the intention to change from IFR to VFR flight, the ATS unit should pass to the pilot, any available meteorological information that makes it likely that flight in VMC cannot be maintained.

G-AB IMC reported in the
vicinity of Kennington

G-AB Roger maintaining IFR

Figure 12.5   Reporting conditions

12.2.3 IFR Departures

At many airports, a single approach control unit handles both arrivals and departures. At busier airports, departures and arrivals may be handled separately by specific arrival and departure control units.

In addition to the ATC route clearance, departing IFR flights may be given departure instructions, in order to provide separation. These may be given in plain language or in the form of a Standard Instrument Departure (SID).

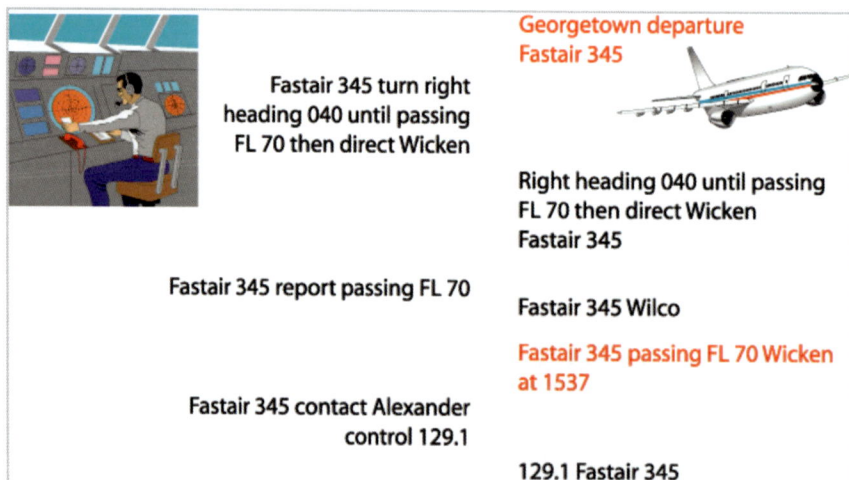

Fastair 345 turn right
heading 040 until passing
FL 70 then direct Wicken

Georgetown departure
Fastair 345

Right heading 040 until passing
FL 70 then direct Wicken
Fastair 345

Fastair 345 report passing FL 70

Fastair 345 Wilco

Fastair 345 passing FL 70 Wicken
at 1537

Fastair 345 contact Alexander
control 129.1

129.1 Fastair 345

Figure 12.6   Departure clearance

12.2.4 IFR Arrivals

Approach control will normally advise, on initial contact, the type of approach to be expected.

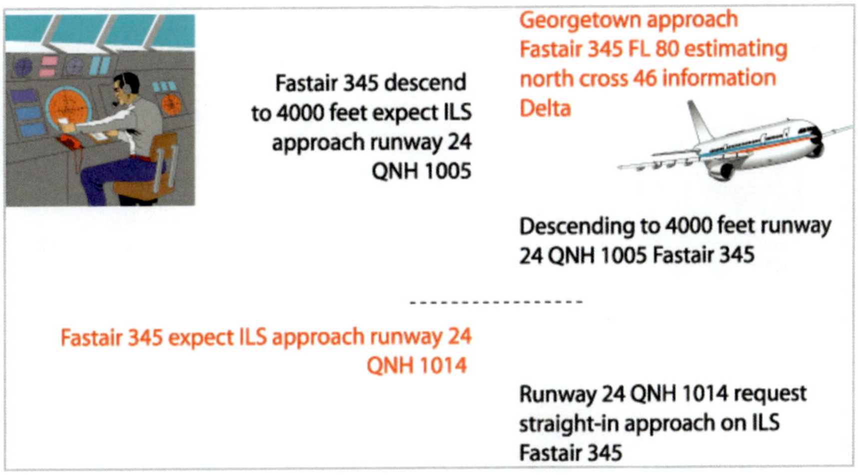

Fastair 345 descend to 4000 feet expect ILS approach runway 24 QNH 1005

Georgetown approach Fastair 345 FL 80 estimating north cross 46 information Delta

Descending to 4000 feet runway 24 QNH 1005 Fastair 345

Fastair 345 expect ILS approach runway 24 QNH 1014

Runway 24 QNH 1014 request straight-in approach on ILS Fastair 345

Figure 12.7   IFR arrival

On occasion, IFR aircraft do not complete the instrument approach procedure, but request permission to make a visual approach. A request for a visual approach does not imply that the aircraft is flying in VMC but only that the specified requirements for a visual approach have been met and that the pilot can maintain visual reference to the terrain.

Normally a holding procedure should be published. However, when the pilot requires a detailed description of the holding procedure based on a facility, the Information should be passed in the following order:
- Fix
- Level
- Inbound track
- Right or left turns
- Time of leg (if necessary)

12.2.5 Position Reporting

Position reports shall contain the following elements of information, except that elements 4), 5) and 6) may be omitted when prescribed on the basis of regional air navigation agreements.
1. Aircraft identification
2. Position
3. Time
4. Level
5. Next position and time over
6. Ensuing significant point

When transmitting time, only the minutes of the hour should normally be required. Each digit should be pronounced separately. However, the hour should be included when any possibility of confusion is likely to arise.

Fastair 345 Wicken 47 FL 330 Marlow 57 Colinton next

Fastair 345 Roger

Figure 12.8   Time

Where adequate flight progress data are available from other sources, such as surveillance radar, flights may be exempted from the requirement to make compulsory position reports.

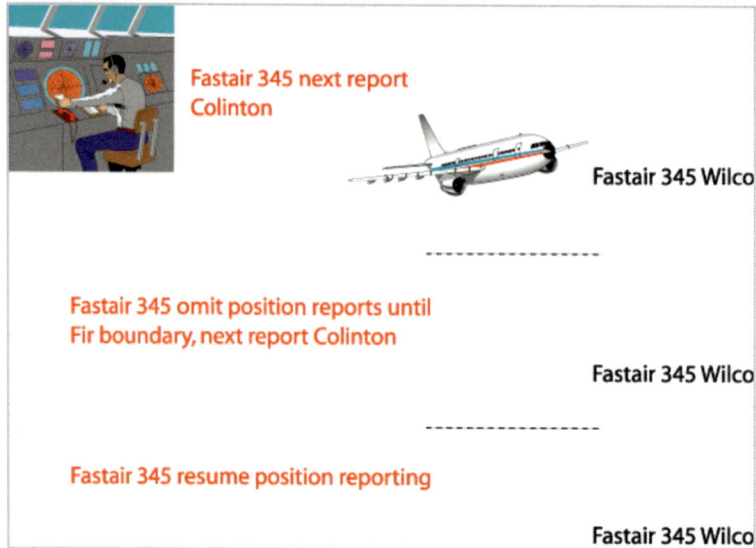

Figure 12.9   Position reports

12.3 Aircraft Call Signs

See *Section 1, 6.5.2 Aircraft call signs* for related information.

An aircraft shall not change its type of call sign or alter its call sign during flight. If there is likelihood that confusion may occur because of similar call signs, an aircraft may be instructed by an air traffic control unit to change the type of its call sign temporarily as an exception using the following procedure:

To instruct an aircraft to change its type of call sign:
CHANGE YOUR CALL SIGN TO (new call sign) [UNTIL FURTHER ADVISED]

To advise an aircraft to revert to the call sign indicated in the flight plan:
REVERT TO FLIGHT PLAN CALL SIGN (call sign) [AT (significant point)].

Aircraft in the heavy wake turbulence category shall include the word "HEAVY" immediately after the aircraft call sign in the initial call to the aerodrome control tower and the approach control unit

12.4 Vertical Position

The vertical position of an aircraft is referred to as follows:
* Flight level – when the standard pressure setting of 1013.25 hPa (29.92 inches Hg) is set on the altimeter subscale
* Altitude – when QNH is set on the altimeter subscale
* Height – when QFE is set on the altimeter subscale

12.5 Level Instructions

The precise phraseology used in the transmission and acknowledgement of climb and descent clearances will vary, depending upon the circumstances, traffic density and nature of the flight operations. However, care must be taken to ensure that misunderstandings are not generated as a consequence of the phraseology employed during these phases of flight. For example, levels may be reported as altitude, height or flight levels, according to the phase of flight and the altimeter setting.

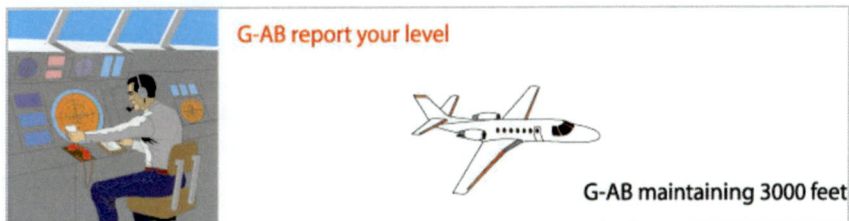

Figure 12.10   Level instructions

In the following examples, the operations of climbing and descending are interchangeable and examples of only one form are given. Once having been given an instruction to climb or descend, a further overriding instruction may be given to a pilot.

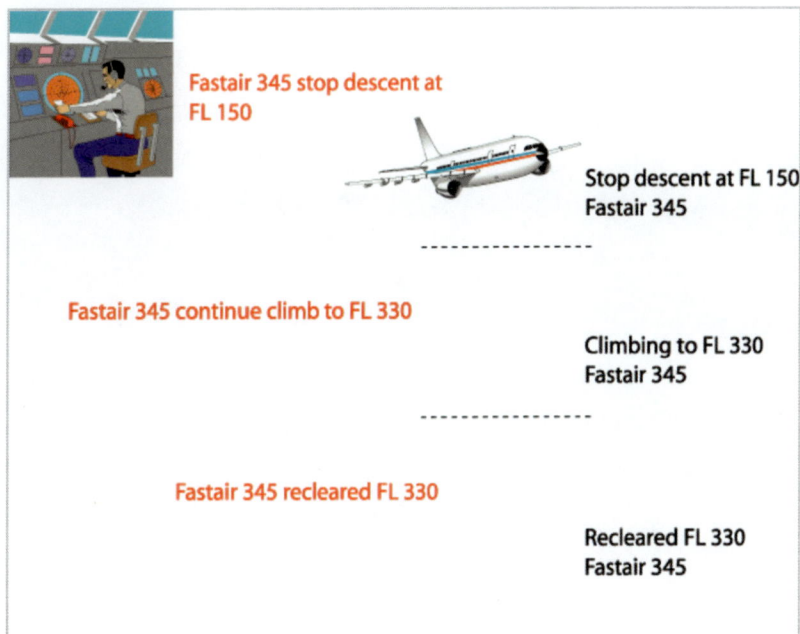

Figure 12.11   Descent instructions

Occasionally for traffic reasons a higher than normal rate of climb or descent may be required.

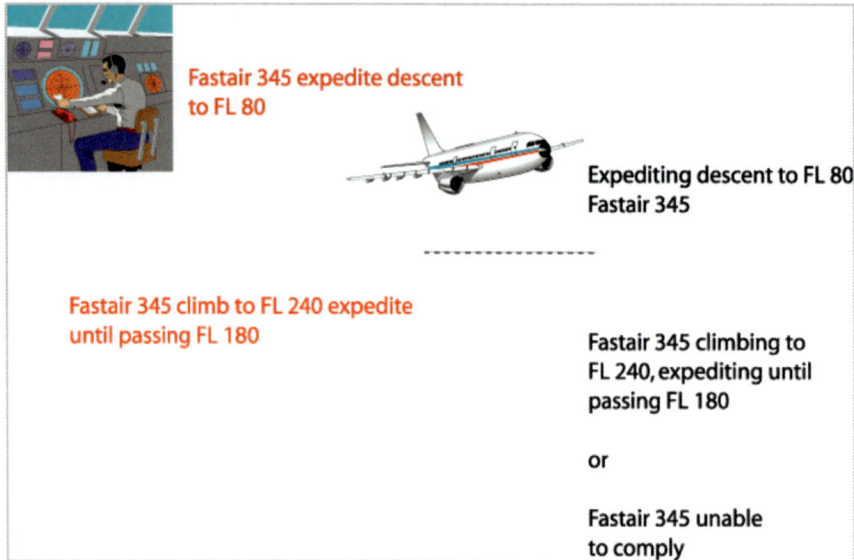

Figure 12.12   Expediting descent

CRANFIELD AVIATION TRAINING SCHOOL LTD. PART-FCL ATO N° 0136
CATS INNOVATION CENTRE, LUTON, Bedfordshire LU2 8DL U.K.

www.catsaviation.com

12-7

Communications

CHAPTER 13
IFR Communication Failure

13.1 Introduction

The following actions should be taken in the case of communication failure on an IFR flight.

If in visual meteorological conditions when communication failure occurs, the aircraft shall:
- continue to fly in visual meteorological conditions
- land at the nearest suitable aerodrome, and
- report its arrival by the most expeditious means, to the appropriate air traffic control unit

According to ICAO:

If in instrument meteorological conditions or when conditions are such that it does not appear feasible to complete the flight in accordance with VMC rules, the aircraft shall:

- unless otherwise prescribed on the basis of regional air navigation agreement, maintain the last assigned speed and level, or minimum flight altitude if higher, for a period of **20 min** following the aircraft's failure to report its position over a compulsory reporting point and thereafter adjust level and speed in accordance with the filed flight plan.

- proceed according to the current flight plan route, to the appropriate designated navigation aid serving the destination aerodrome and, when required to ensure compliance below, hold over this aid until commencement of descent.

- commence descent from the navigation aid specified in b) at, or as close as possible to, the expected approach time last received and acknowledged. If no expected approach time has been received and acknowledged, commence descent at or as close as possible to the estimated time of arrival from the current flight plan.

- complete a normal instrument approach procedure as specified for the designated approach aid, and

- land, if possible, within 30 min after the estimated time of arrival specified above or the last acknowledged expected approach time, whichever is later

The following procedure is used in Europe for IFR radio failures:

In Europe, a regional air navigation agreement has been made where a departing controlled IFR flight operating in IMC, having acknowledged an initial or intermediate clearance to climb to a level other than the one specified in the current flight plan for the en-route phase of the flight, and experiencing two-way communication failure should, if no time limit or geographical limit was included in the climb clearance, maintain for a period of **3 min** the level to which is was cleared and then continue its flight in accordance with the current flight plan

CHAPTER 14
PAN Medical Procedure

14.1 Aircraft used for medical transports

For the purpose of announcing and identifying aircraft used for medical transports, a transmission of the radiotelephony urgency signal PAN PAN, preferably spoken three times, shall be followed by the radiotelephony signal for medical transports MAY-DEE-CAL.

E.g. PAN PAN, PAN PAN, PAN PAN, MAY-DEE-CAL

The use of the signals described above indicates that the message which follows concerns a protected medical transport, pursuant to the 1949 Geneva Conventions and Additional Protocols. The message shall convey the following data:

- the call sign or other recognised means of identification of the medical transports
- position of the medical transports
- number and type of medical transports
- intended route
- estimated time en route and of departure and arrival, as appropriate; and any other information such as flight altitude, radio frequencies guarded, languages used, and secondary surveillance radar modes and codes.

CHAPTER 15
Meteorological Information

15.1 Runway Visual Range

When transmitting the runway visual range the words "RUNWAY VISUAL RANGE" or the abbreviation RVR should be used, followed by the runway number, the position for multiple readings if necessary and the RVR value(s). Where multiple RVR observations are available, they are always transmitted commencing with the reading for the touchdown zone.

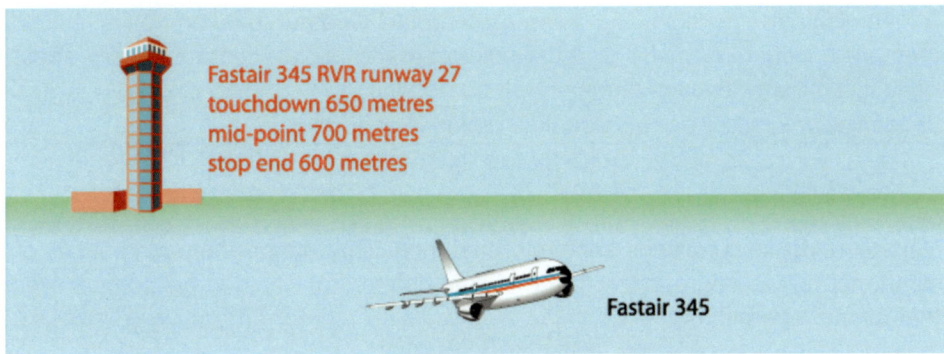

Fastair 345 RVR runway 27
touchdown 650 metres
mid-point 700 metres
stop end 600 metres

Fastair 345

Figure 15.1   RVR

15.2 Braking Action

Braking action (friction coefficients) are reported in the following format:

Measured/calculated coefficient	or	Estimated surface friction
0.40 and above		GOOD - 5
0.39 to 0.36		GOOD/MEDIUM- 4
0.35 to 0.30		MEDIUM - 3
0.29 to 0.26		MEDIUM/POOR - 2
0.25 and below		POOR - 1
9 – unreliable		UNRELIABLE - 9

15.3 Aircraft Observations and Reports

The following aircraft meteorological observations shall be made:
* routine aircraft observations
* special aircraft observations
* aircraft observations during climb-out and approach, and
* other aircraft observations on request

15.3.1 Aircraft Routine Meteorological Observations

Routine meteorological observations shall be made in relation to those air traffic services reporting points or intervals:
* at which the applicable air traffic services procedures require routine position reports, and
* which are those separated by distances corresponding most closely to intervals of one hour of flying time

An aircraft shall be exempted from making routine observations when:
- the flight duration is 2 h or less, or
- the aircraft is at a distance equivalent to less than one hour of flying time from the next intended point of landing, or
- the altitude of the flight path is below 1500 m (5000')

15.3.2 Aircraft Special Meteorological Observations

Special meteorological observations shall be made by all aircraft whenever:
- severe turbulence or severe icing is encountered, or
- moderate turbulence, hail or cumulonimbus clouds are encountered during transonic or supersonic flight, or
- volcanic ash cloud is observed or encountered, or
- other meteorological conditions, for example enroute weather phenomena specified for SIGMET messages are encountered, which, in the opinion of the pilot-in-command may affect the safety or markedly affect the efficiency of other aircraft operations, or
- pre-eruption volcanic activity or a volcanic eruption is observed.

15.3.3 Observations made during climb out or approach

Observations of meteorological conditions encountered during climb-out or approach phases of flight shall be made by all aircraft, not previously reported to the pilot-in-command, which in his opinion are likely to affect the safety of other aircraft operations.

15.3.4 Reporting Procedures

Routine aircraft observations shall be reported during flight as routine air-reports at times of transmission of the associated position report. Special aircraft observations shall be reported during flight as special air-reports, as soon after they have been made as is practicable

Aircraft observations made during climb-out and approach phase of flight shall be reported as soon, as is practicable.

15.3.5 AIREP messages

The elements contained in air-reports and their order in the AIREP message shall be:

1. Aircraft identification	
2. Position	
3. Time	Section 1
4. Flight level or altitude	Position Information
5. Next position and time over	
6. Ensuing significant point	
7. Estimated time of arrival	Section 2
8. Endurance	Operational information
9. Air temperature	
10. Wind	
11. Turbulence	Section 3
12. Aircraft icing	Meteorological information
13. Supplementary information	

The elements contained in special air-reports of pre-eruption volcanic activity, a volcanic eruption or volcanic ash cloud and their order in the AIREP message shall be:

- Aircraft identification
- Position
- Time
- Flight level or altitude
- Volcanic activity observed
- Air temperature
- Wind
- Supplementary information

CRANFIELD AVIATION TRAINING SCHOOL LTD. PART-FCL ATO N° 0136
CATS INNOVATION CENTRE, LUTON, Bedfordshire LU2 8DL U.K.

www.catsaviation.com

15-3

Communications

IFR COMMUNICATIONS Self Assessment Test 01

1. An aeronautical fixed service is:
A) A telecommunication service between specified fixed points, provided primarily for the safety of air navigation and for the regular, efficient and economical operation of air services
B) A world wide system of aeronautical fixed services provided for the exchange of messages and / or digital data
C) The fixed manoeuvring area of an apron
D) The fixed specified path to be flown by an aircraft operating in the vicinity of an aerodrome

2. SQUAWK CHARLIE means:
A) Select Standby
B) Select pressure altitude transmission
C) De-select all modes except mode C
D) Select 2000

3. CHECK ID SQUAWK means:
A) Use the alternative transponder
B) Say again your position and set previous code
C) For a mode S equipped aircraft check identification setting
D) Confirm mode A is set on the transponder

4. A reporting point is a:
A) Specific point on the NATS system
B) Location concerning a VOR beacon on the centreline of an airway
C) Specific point on a coast line feature
D) A specific geographical location in relation to which the position of an aircraft can be reported

5. A radar approach is:
A) An approach, executed by an aircraft, under the direction of a radar controller
B) An approach, executed by an aircraft, under the direction of a local controller and assisted by radar
C) Not approved for the direction of 'heavy' aircraft
D) None of the above

6. Radar vectoring means that:
A) An aircraft is under specific control of a radar runway control system
B) Navigational guidance is being provided to aircraft in the form of specific headings, based on the use of radar
C) Mode C is in operation
D) The ILS will be flown with radar monitoring

7. Visual meteorological conditions (VMC) can be defined as:
A) Conditions suitable for a radar vectored approach to a fixing point
B) Those conditions which allow a visual approach to a runway which is temporally closed
C) Those conditions expressed in terms of visibility, distance from cloud, and ceiling, equal or better than specified minima
D) Those conditions which prohibit instrument traffic from approaching the a runway other than by setting the QDM

8. When flying at a flight level, the altimeter pressure setting scale (hPa or in Hg) is set to:
A) 1013.2 inches Hg; 29.92 feet Hg
B) 1013 hPa; 29.92 inches Hg
C) 1013.2 feet; 29.92 hPa
D) 1013.2 hPa; 29.92 inches Hg

CRANFIELD AVIATION TRAINING SCHOOL LTD. PART-FCL ATO N° 0136
CATS CATS INNOVATION CENTRE, LUTON, Bedfordshire LU2 8DL U.K.   www.catsaviation.com

15-4

Communications

9. Below the transition level the altimeter sub scale is set to:
A) QFE
B) 1013.2 hPa
C) QNH
D) QGH

10. On a surveillance radar approach (SRA) a pilot is given:
A) Heights from touchdown and the surface wind
B) Distances and vectors to achieve a circling approach at 5 NM intervals
C) Distances from touchdown, advisory altitude or height information, and azimuth instructions
D) Advisory height and distances from touchdown only

11. An SRA can be terminated at less than:
A) 5 NM (preferably 6 NM) and the controllers transmissions should not be interrupted for periods of more than 10 s
B) 2 NM from touchdown and the controllers transmissions should not be interrupted for periods of more than 8 s
C) 2 NM from touchdown and the controllers transmissions should not be interrupted for periods more than 5 s. Once the aircraft is within 4 NM, pilot replies are not expected
D) 2 NM from touchdown and the controllers transmissions should not be interrupted for periods more than 5 s. Once the aircraft is within 5 NM, pilot replies are not expected

12. On a precision radar approach a pilot is given:
A) Heading instructions, altitudes relative to the glideslope and corrective action instructions if the aircraft is too high or too low
B) Height correction instructions only
C) Heading corrections only
D) Heading instructions and altitudes relative to the glideslope

13. On occasion, IFR traffic may opt to carry out a visual approach. This means that:
A) The aircraft is now flying in VMC
B) The specified requirements for a visual approach have been met and that the pilot can maintain visual reference to the terrain
C) The aircraft is still IMC but that VFR conditions are currently being met
D) IFR traffic is leaving the zone under VMC conditions

14. In a radar environment, headings are given in:
A) Degrees True
B) Degrees Grid
C) Degrees Magnetic
D) Degrees True or Magnetic by agreement between the controller and the aircraft commander

15. Runway visual range (RVR) is the:
A) Length of the runway in metres as defined by the ILS localiser sweep
B) Length of the greatest extent of poor visibility measured down the centre line of the runway
C) The range over which the pilot of an aircraft on the centre line can see the runway surface markings or the lights delineating or identifying its centre line
D) Distance is feet between the runway threshold and the nearest obstacle which may affect the length of the take off run

16. ATZ is an abbreviation for:
A) Air terminal zone
B) Aerodrome terminal zone
C) Aircraft terminal zone
D) Aerodrome traffic zone

17. VORTAC is a facility which provides:
A) Bearing and range
B) Bearing only
C) Range only
D) VOR = range and TACAN = bearing

18. An aircraft UHF installation provides a frequency range of:
A) 300 to 3000 MHz
B) 300 to 3000 kHz
C) 300 to 30 000 MHz
D) 300 to 3000 Hz

19. Aircraft in the heavy wake turbulence category:
A) Shall prefix all radio transmissions to air traffic units with the word HEAVY
B) Shall include the word HEAVY immediately after the aircraft call sign in the initial call to the aerodrome control tower and the approach control unit
C) Shall immediately specify the degree of turbulence about to be generated prior to a heavy weight take-off
D) By mutual agreement with the relevant air traffic unit, prefix all radio calls with the word HEAVY

20. In the phonetic alphabet, the word thousand is pronounced:
A) Thousand
B) Mill
C) Tou-sand
D) Mb

IFR COMMUNICATIONS Self Assessment Test 01 ANSWERS

1	A
2	B
3	C
4	D
5	A
6	B
7	C
8	D
9	C
10	C
11	C
12	A
13	B
14	C
15	C
16	D
17	A
18	A
19	B
20	C

CRANFIELD AVIATION TRAINING SCHOOL LTD. PART-FCL ATO N° 0136
CATS INNOVATION CENTRE, LUTON, Bedfordshire LU2 8DL U.K.

www.catsaviation.com

15-7

Communications

CATS

IFR COMMUNICATIONS Self Assessment Test 02

1. The call sign for an approach control facility is:
A) CONTROL
B) ARRIVAL
C) TOWER
D) APPROACH

2. The call sign for an approach control arrivals facility is:
A) CONTROL
B) ARRIVAL
C) TOWER
D) APPROACH

3. The call sign for a direction finding facility is:
A) GROUND
B) DF
C) HOMER
D) TOWER

4. According to ICAO, the call sign for a precision approach radar facility is:
A) PPA
B) ARRIVAL
C) RADAR
D) PRECISION

5. The SELCAL system allows for the:
A) Selective calling of one aircraft from another on the company frequency
B) Selective calling of an individual aircraft by a ground station
C) Selective calling of individual ground stations from an aircraft, via chimes and lights
D) Selective calling from man aircraft to a ship on the maritime distress frequency

6. An aircraft shall be exempted from making routine observations (AIREP) when:
A) The flight time is 2 h or less, the aircraft is less than one hours' flight from the intended point of landing or, the flight path is below 5000' (1500 m)
B) The flight time is 2 h or less only
C) The flight time remaining to destination is 3 h
D) The aircraft is at 8000' or below

7. Name two occasions when special observations (SPECI) may be transmitted by an aircraft:
A) Calls for company use only and routine position reports
B) Passenger handling information which may be useful for the next leg of a flight and time of departure from previous station
C) Animal quarantine requests and enquiries concerning the validity of inoculation certificates
D) Severe turbulence is encountered or the presence of volcanic ash is observed

8. A position report shall consist of the following information:
A) Aircraft identification, position, time, level, next position and time over....., the ensuing significant point
B) Aircraft identification, next position and time over next point and fuel remaining
C) Aircraft identification, time and next position
D) Aircraft identification, time over next point and fuel remaining

9. Which of the following statements is correct:
A) An aircraft must always read back an airways clearance immediately it is received
B) A QDL call is made when an aircraft requires the distance from a direction finding station
C) An aircraft can be instructed to STANDBY on a frequency when it is intended that the ATS will initiate further communication and MONITOR a frequency on which information is being broadcast
D) When MAYDAY action is taken, it must be initiated on the distress frequency and subsequently changed to the frequency allocated by the controlling authority

10. Clearance delivery provides:
A) Permission to taxi and taxi routes
B) Airways clearances
C) Aerodrome departures information
D) Flight information services

11. If a pilot changes from IFR to VFR, the controlling ATS unit should:
A) Pass any meteorological information that makes it likely that flight in VMC cannot be maintained
B) Allocate a flight level which will allow VMC to be maintained
C) Cancel all further requirements to pass position reports
D) Ensure that 1013 hPa is set

12. Routine observation reports shall be made in relation to those air traffic services reporting points or intervals:
A) At which the applicable air traffic services procedures require routine position reports only
B) At which the applicable air traffic services procedures require routine position reports and also which are separated by distances corresponding most closely to intervals of one hours flying time
C) Provided the flight time is greater than 4 hours and that there is at least one hours flight time to the current alternate aerodrome
D) None of the above

13. When an RVR is transmitted:
A) It shall only consist of a reading at the runway threshold only. RVR are transmitted in meters
B) The message content shall consist of the runway number and the RVR. Where multiple RVR readings are passed, the first one is that at the touch down zone. RVR are transmitted in metres
C) Readings are in feet and taxi way readings are included together with the status of the VASIS
D) RVR information is never provided unless requested

14. An AIREP message shall consist of the following elements:
A) Position information, number of passengers on board and fuel remaining
B) Fuel remaining, next reporting point and time, temperature and flight level
C) Position information, operational information and meteorological information
D) Position information, meteorological information and fuel remaining

15. Above the transition level:
A) QFE is set
B) QNH is set
C) The RPS is set
D) 1013 hPa is set

16. If a communication failure occurs whilst in IMC, the following actions, in general terms, should be taken:
A) Maintain the last assigned speed and FL for 20 min then maintain flight plan route keeping as close to the timings as possible. If a transponder is fitted, set 7600
B) No special action is required
C) Climb to the greatest altitude as possible and thereafter cruise for range maintaining, as far as possible, the flight plane route and timings
D) Set 7600 on the transponder and land as soon as possible

17. The correct phraseology for pushback is as follows:
A) Pilot: CLEARED TO PUSHBACK
    Ground crew: BRAKES OFF, PUSHING BACK
B) Pilot: STANDBY FOR PUSHBACK, BRAKES OFF
    Ground crew   STANDING BY, BRAKES OFF, PUSHING BACK
C) Pilot: READY FOR PUSHBACK
    Ground crew: CONFIRM BRAKES RELEASED
D) None of the above

18. If an engine fire occurs in flight, the transponder is set to:
A) 7600
B) 7700
C) 7500
D) 7500 and Mode Charlie

19. When a detailed description of a holding pattern is requested, the information shall be passed in the following order:
A) Level, right or left hand turns, time of leg and fix
B) Right or left hand turns, fix, time of leg and level
C) Time of leg, left or right hand turns, fix and level
D) Fix, level, inbound track, right or left hand turns and time of leg (if necessary)

IFR COMMUNICATIONS Self Assessment Test 02 ANSWERS

1	D
2	B
3	C
4	D
5	B
6	A
7	D
8	A
9	C
10	B
11	A
12	B
13	B
14	C
15	D
16	A
17	C
18	B
19	D

INDEX

AAL	1-4
ACC	1-4
Accuracy of Bearings and Positions	3-1
ACKNOWLEDGE	6-1
ADF	1-4
ADR	1-4
Aerodrome control radio station	1-1
Aerodrome control service	1-1
Aerodrome traffic	1-1
Aerodrome traffic circuit	1-1
Aeronautical fixed service	1-2
Aeronautical fixed telecommunication network (AFTN)	1-2
Aeronautical mobile service	1-2, 2-1
Aeronautical station	1-1
AFFIRM	6-1
AFIS	1-4
AGL	1-4
AIP	1-4
Air traffic	1-2
Air traffic control clearance	1-2
Air traffic service	1-2
Air traffic services unit	1-2
AIRAC	1-4
AIRBORNE	6-23
AIREP	15-2
Airway	1-2
AIS	1-5
ALL STATIONS	6-19
alphabet	5-1
Altitude	1-2
AMSL	1-5
APPROACH	6-18
Approach control service	1-2
APPROVED	6-1
Apron	1-2
APRON	6-18
Area control centre	1-2
ARRIVAL	6-18
ATC	1-5
ATD	1-5
ATIS	1-5, 6-4, 8-1
ATS	1-5
Attenuation	11-3
ATZ	1-5
Automatic terminal information service	1-2
Bearings	3-2
Blind transmission	1-1
Braking Action	15-1
BREAK	6-1
BREAK BREAK	6-1
Broadcast	1-1
Call Signs	6-17, 12-5
CANCEL	6-1
CAVOK	1-5, 8-1
CHECK	6-1
Circuit	6-9
Clearance	6-22
Clearance limit	1-2, 6-4
CLEARED	6-1
Communication Failure	9-1, 13-1
Conditional clearances	6-7
CONFIRM	6-1
CONTACT	6-1
CONTROL	6-18
Control zone	1-3
Controlled airspace	1-3
CORRECT	6-1
CORRECTION	6-1, 6-20
CTR	1-5
DEGREES	6-2
DELIVERY	6-18
DEPARTURE	6-18, 6-23
Direction Finding	4-1
DISPATCH	6-18
DISREGARD	6-1
Distress	10-1
Distress Messages	4-1
DME	1-5
EET	1-5
Essential Aerodrome Information	6-15
ETA	1-5
ETD	1-5
Expected approach time	1-3
FIC	1-5
FINAL	6-12
FIR	1-5
FIS	1-5
Flight information centre	1-3
Flight level	1-3
Flight plan	1-3, 12-2
Flight Regularity Messages	4-2
Flight Safety Messages	4-1
frequency	11-2
Frequency Bands	11-4
GCA	1-5
GO AHEAD	6-1
Go around	6-14
GROUND	6-18
Ground Waves	11-3
H24	1-5
Heading	1-3
HECTOPASCALS	6-2
Hertz	11-2
HF	1-5
Hijack	7-2
HJ	1-5
HN	1-5
Holding point	1-3
Holding procedure	1-3
HOMER	6-18
HOW DO YOU READ	6-1

CRANFIELD AVIATION TRAINING SCHOOL LTD. PART-FCL ATO N° 0136
CATS INNOVATION CENTRE, LUTON, Bedfordshire LU2 8DL U.K.

www.catsaviation.com

i

Communications

I SAY AGAIN 6-1
IFR 1-5
IFR flight.. 1-3
ILS.. 1-5, 6-2
IMC 1-5
IMMEDIATELY 6-2
INFO 1-5
INFORMATION... 6-18
INS 1-5
Instrument meteorological conditions 1-3
Letters 5-1
Level 1-3
Level Instructions 12-6
line of sight.. 11-3, 11-5
LONG FINAL 6-12
LORAN... 1-5
Manoeuvring area...................................... 1-3
MAYDAY.. 4-1, 10-1
MET 1-5
METAR 1-5
Meteorological Messages 4-2
Missed approach procedure 1-3
MLS.. 1-5
MNPS... 1-5
MONITOR... 6-1
Movement area 1-4
NDB 1-5
NEGATIVE.. 6-1, 6-24
NIL 1-5
NOTAM.. 1-5
Numbers 5-2
OUT 6-1
OVER.. 6-1
PAN Medical 14-1
PAN PAN 4-1, 10-1
PAN PAN MEDICAL 4-1
PAPI... 1-5
phonetic alphabet 5-1
Position Reporting 12-4
Positions 3-2
PRECISION 6-18
Precision Radar Approach.......................... 7-3
Priority of messages 4-1
pushback 12-1
Q-Codes... 3-1
QDL.. 3-1
QDM... 3-1
QDR.. 3-1
QFE... 1-5, 3-1
QGE.. 3-1
QGH.. 3-1
QNH.. 1-5, 3-1, 6-2
QTE... 3-1
QTF... 3-1
QUJ... 3-1
RADAR 6-18
Radar approach 1-4
RADAR CONTROL..................................... 7-1

Radar identification 1-4
Radar vectoring... 1-4
RADIO 6-18
RADIO CHECK 6-21
Radio Communication Discipline 2-1
Radio failure... 7-2
RCC 1-5
Readback... 1-1, 6-1, 6-22
RECLEARED 6-1
Reflection 11-4
Refraction 11-4
REPORT 6-1
Reporting point.. 1-4
REQUEST 6-1
RNAV 1-5
ROGER 6-1
Runway visual range........................... 1-4, 15-1
RVR.. 1-5, 6-2
SAY AGAIN.. 6-2, 6-19
Secondary Surveillance Radar 7-1
SELCAL 1-5
SID 1-5
SIGMET 1-5
Sky Waves 11-3
SNOWTAM 1-5
SPEAK SLOWER 6-2
SPECIAL.. 1-5, 15-2
Special VFR 6-17
SQUAWK 7-1
SSR 1-6
SSR codes 7-2
SST 1-6
STAND BY 6-2
STAR.. 1-6
STOPPING 6-9
stuck microphone 5-3
SURFACE... 6-2
Surveillance Radar Approach 7-2
TACAN 1-6
TAF 1-6
TAKE OFF 6-23
Take-Off Procedures................................... 6-5
Taxi Instructions 6-4
Telecommunication..................................... 1-1
Time 5-3
TMA... 1-6
Touchdown 1-4
TOWER.. 6-18
Track 1-4
transceiver 2-1
'TRANSMITTING BLIND............................. 9-1
Transmitting Techniques 5-3
UHF.. 1-6
UIR... 1-6
UNABLE TO COMPLY 6-25
Urgency.. 10-1
Urgency Messages 4-1
UTA.. 1-6

UTC.. 1-6, 5-3
VASIS 1-6
VDF 1-6
VERIFY 6-2
Vertical Position 12-5
VFR.. 1-6
VFR flight 1-4
VHF 1-6
VIP 1-6
VISIBILITY 6-2

Visual approach 1-4
Visual meteorological conditions 1-4
VMC 1-6
VOLMET 1-6, 8-1
VOR 1-6
VORTAC 1-6
Wavelength 11-2
WILCO 6-2
WORDS TWICE... 6-2